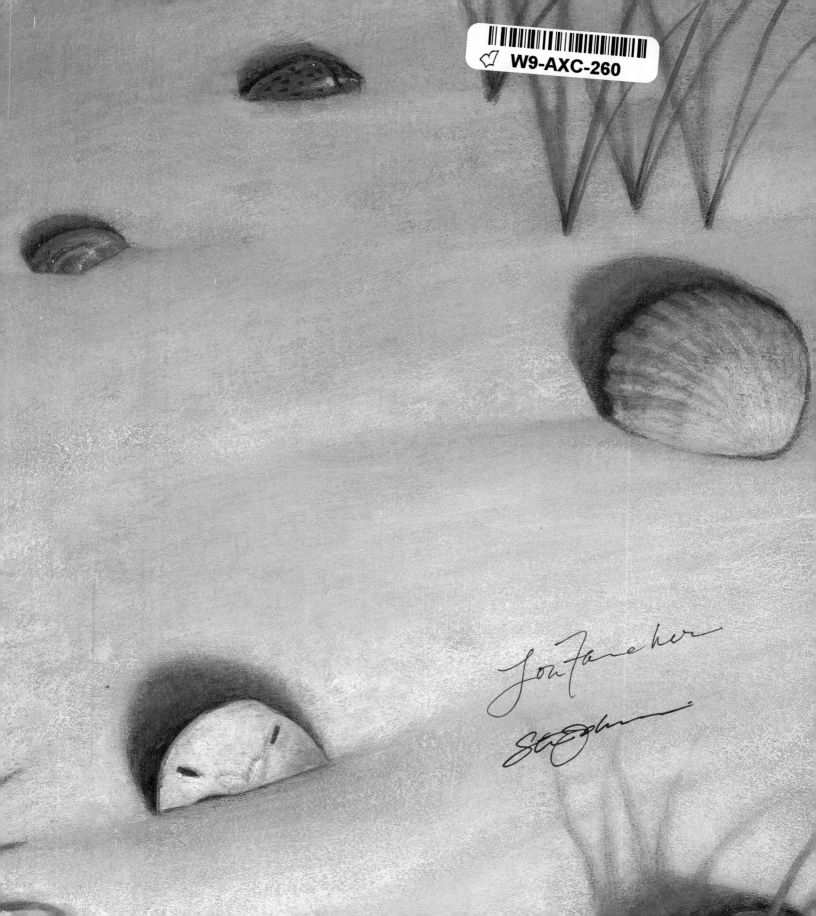

Living Colors

Harcourt Brace & Company

Living Colors

Senior Authors

Roger C. Farr

Dorothy S. Strickland

Authors

Richard F. Abrahamson ✦ Alma Flor Ada ✦ Barbara Bowen Coulter

Bernice E. Cullinan ✦ Margaret A. Gallego

W. Dorsey Hammond

Nancy Roser ✦ Junko Yokota ✦ Hallie Kay Yopp

Senior Consultant

Asa G. Hilliard III

Consultants

Kanani Choy ✦ Lee Bennett Hopkins ✦ Stephen Krashen ✦ Rosalia Salinas

Harcourt Brace & Company

Orlando Atlanta Austin Boston San Francisco Chicago Dallas New York Toronto London

Printed in the United States of America

ISBN 0-15-306400-5+

1 2 3 4 5 6 7 8 9 10   048   99 98 97 96

Dear Reader,

Did you ever look around you at the colors outside? Trees, buildings, dirt and rocks, grass and flowers, the sky, the sea, and even people all hold within them the living colors of the earth.

In **Living Colors**, you will find answers to these questions and more. How can a bat win a ball game? How can a boy help his grandfather's dream come true? When could there ever be too many tamales?

You will read stories that began in Venezuela and Vietnam, in Panama, and even from as far away as Pluto!

We hope you like them all.

Sincerely,

The Authors

The Authors

THEME

FAMILIES THAT CARE AND SHARE

CONTENTS

Theme
IN THE NIGHT SKY

Contents

Dare to **Dream**

Contents

THEME

FAMILIES THAT CARE AND SHARE

What kinds of things do you do for fun with your family?
Do you like to have relatives visit? Families often
share happy times. What are some happy times
you've shared with your family?

THEME

FAMILIES THAT CARE AND SHARE

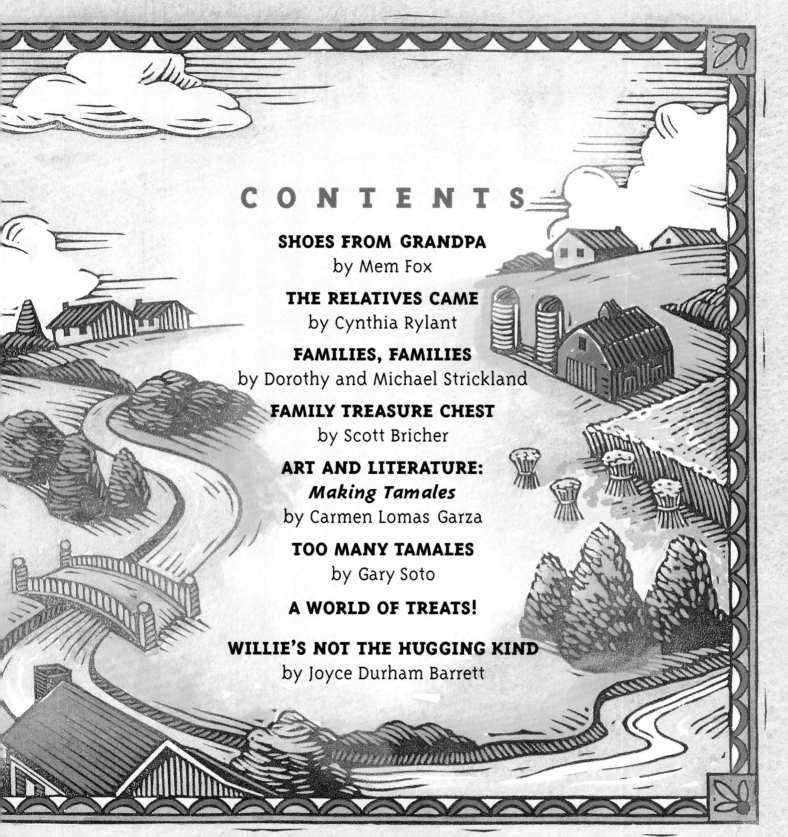

CONTENTS

BOOKSHELF

Who's Who in My Family?

written and illustrated
by Loreen Leedy

Join Ms. Fox's class and find out how each person in your family is related to you.

Signatures Library

Award-Winning Author

JoJo's Flying Side Kick

written and illustrated
by Brian Pinkney

Will JoJo pass the test in her Tae Kwon Do class? How does her family help her?

Signatures Library

Award-Winning Author

At the Beach
by Huy Voun Lee

A mother teaches her son to write in Chinese while they spend a day at the beach.

A Birthday Basket for Tía
by Pat Mora

Cecilia finds the perfect gift for her great-aunt's birthday.
Award-Winning Author

Tomorrow on Rocky Pond
by Lynn Reiser

A family looks forward to a fishing trip at Rocky Pond.
Children's Choice

Late one summer Jessie's father invited all the family over for a barbecue.

19

When Grandpa saw Jessie he stood back and said, "My, how you've grown! You'll need a new pair of shoes this winter, and I'll buy them."

"Thanks a lot, Grandpa," said Jessie.

Then her dad said,
"I'll buy you some socks from the local shops,
to go with the shoes from Grandpa."

And her mom said,
"I'll buy you a skirt that won't show the dirt,
to go with the socks from the local shops,
to go with the shoes from Grandpa."

25

And her cousin said,
"I'll look for a blouse with ribbons and bows,
to go with the skirt that won't show the dirt,
to go with the socks from the local shops,
to go with the shoes from Grandpa."

And her sister said,
"I'll get you a sweater when the weather gets wetter,
to go with the blouse with ribbons and bows,
to go with the skirt that won't show the dirt,
to go with the socks from the local shops,
to go with the shoes from Grandpa."

And her grandma said,
"I'll find you a coat you could wear on a boat,
to go with the sweater when the weather gets wetter,
to go with the blouse with ribbons and bows,
to go with the skirt that won't show the dirt,
to go with the socks from the local shops,
to go with the shoes from Grandpa."

And her aunt said,
"I'll knit you a scarf that'll make us all laugh,
to go with the coat you could wear on a boat,
to go with the sweater when the weather gets wetter,
to go with the blouse with ribbons and bows,

to go with the skirt that won't show the dirt,
to go with the socks from the local shops,
to go with the shoes from Grandpa."

And her brother said,
"I'll find you a hat you can put on like that,
to go with the scarf that'll make us all laugh,
to go with the coat you could wear on a boat,
to go with the sweater when the weather gets wetter,
to go with the blouse with ribbons and bows,

to go with the skirt that won't show the dirt,
to go with the socks from the local shops,
to go with the shoes from Grandpa."

And her uncle said,
"I'll buy you some mittens that are softer than kittens,
to go with the hat you can put on like that,
to go with the scarf that'll make us all laugh,
to go with the coat you could wear on a boat,

to go with the sweater when the weather gets wetter,
to go with the blouse with ribbons and bows,
to go with the skirt that won't show the dirt,
to go with the socks from the local shops,
to go with the shoes from Grandpa."

And Jessie said,
"You're all so kind that I hate to be mean,
but please, would one of you buy me some jeans?"

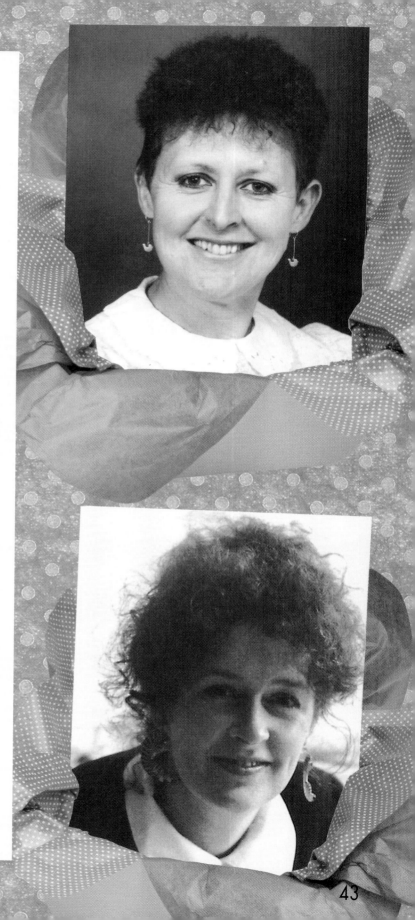

MEM FOX

Mem Fox was born in Australia, but she grew up in Africa. She loved to climb trees, ride bikes, and play football. She also loved to read and write. She wrote her first story when she was ten years old.

Now, she writes books for children because she wants *you* to enjoy reading. Her ideas come from things that happened in her life.

PATRICIA MULLINS

Art was Patricia Mullins's favorite subject in school. She especially liked drawing animals. She liked making animals from paper, cloth scraps, or anything she could find. She also enjoyed going to puppet shows. Can you find puppets in the story?

Response

RIP IT UP

For *Shoes from Grandpa*, Patricia Mullins made collages from torn paper and bits of cloth. You can make a collage, too!

You will need:

construction paper

glue

feathers, yarn, buttons, cloth, and other small objects

1. Think of a person, animal, or place.
2. Tear pieces of construction paper. Move them around on a big sheet of paper until you like your picture.
3. Glue the pieces down.
4. Add bits of cloth or other decorations.

One day I walked everywhere. I walked to Joey's house to see the new puppies.

44

One day I walked everywhere. I walked to Joey's house to see the new puppies. I walked to the corner store to buy some milk.

MAKE UP A STORY

Each part of "Shoes from Grandpa" adds something to the part that comes before it. Work with a group to make up a story like that.

1. Decide what your story will be about. Think of a good beginning sentence.

2. One person says that sentence and adds another sentence. Each person repeats the story and adds another part.

WHAT DO YOU THINK?

- How did "Shoes from Grandpa" start? How did it end?

- How do you think Jessie's relatives might answer her question at the end of the story? How would *you* answer her question?

45

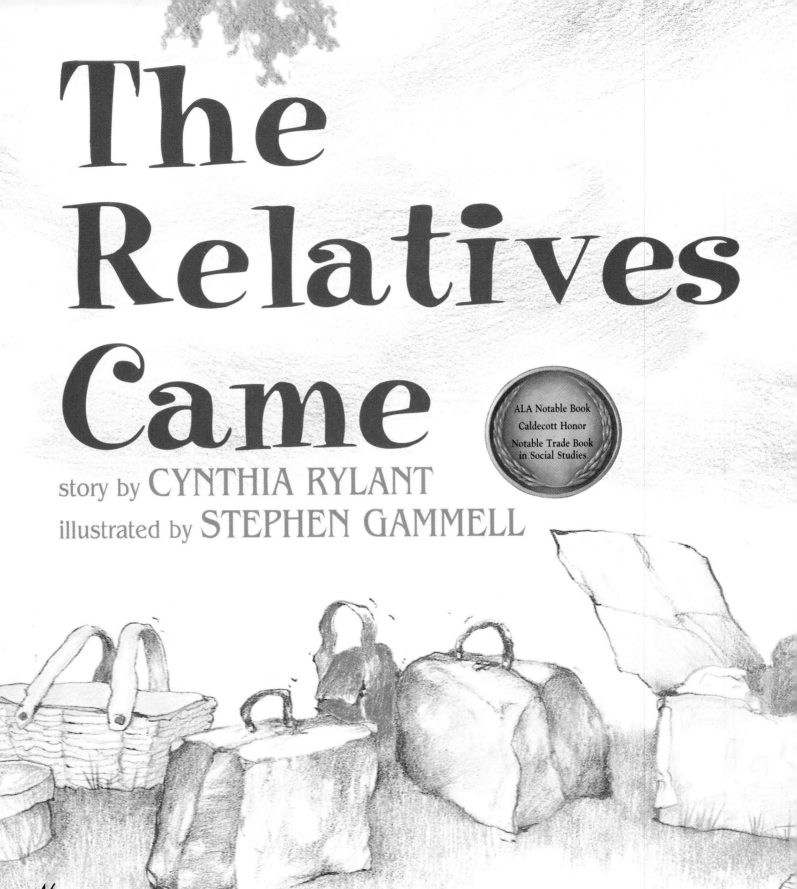

The Relatives Came

story by CYNTHIA RYLANT

illustrated by STEPHEN GAMMELL

ALA Notable Book

Caldecott Honor

Notable Trade Book
in Social Studies

It was in the summer of the year when the relatives came. They came up from Virginia. They left when their grapes were nearly purple enough to pick, but not quite.

They had an old station wagon that smelled like a real
car, and in it they put an ice chest full of soda pop
and some boxes of crackers and some bologna sandwiches,
and up they came—from Virginia.

They left at four in the morning when it was still dark,
before even the birds were awake.

They drove all day long and into the night, and while they
traveled along they looked at the strange houses
and different mountains and they thought
about their almost purple grapes back home.
They thought about Virginia—
but they thought about us, too. Waiting for them.

So they drank up all their pop and ate up all their crackers and traveled up all those miles until finally they pulled into our yard.

50

Then it was hugging time. Talk about hugging!
Those relatives just passed us all around their
car, pulling us against their wrinkled Virginia
clothes, crying sometimes. They hugged us for hours.

Then it was into the house and so much laughing and
shining faces and hugging in the doorways. You'd have to
go through at least four different hugs to get from the
kitchen to the front room. Those relatives!

And finally after a big supper two or three times around
until we all got a turn at the table, there was quiet talk
and we were in twos and threes through the house.

The relatives weren't particular about beds, which was good
since there weren't any extras, so a few squeezed in with us
and the rest slept on the floor, some with their arms
thrown over the closest person, or some with an arm across one person
and a leg across another.

It was different, going to sleep with all that new breathing in the house.

The relatives stayed for weeks and weeks. They helped us tend the garden and they fixed any broken things they could find.

They ate up all our strawberries and melons, then promised we
could eat up all their grapes and peaches when we came to Virginia.

But none of us thought about Virginia much. We were so busy
hugging and eating and breathing together.

Finally, after a long time, the relatives loaded up their ice chest
and headed back to Virginia at four in the morning.
We stood there in our pajamas and waved them off in the dark.
    We watched the relatives disappear down the road,
then we crawled back into our beds that felt too big and too quiet.
We fell asleep.

And the relatives drove on, all day long and into the night,
and while they traveled along they looked at the strange houses
and different mountains and they thought about their
dark purple grapes waiting at home in Virginia.

But they thought about us, too. Missing them. And they missed us.

And when they were finally home in Virginia,
they crawled into their silent, soft beds and dreamed
about the next summer.

CYNTHIA RYLANT

Sometimes Cynthia Rylant's stories are made-up. Other times, she writes about things that really happened. *The Relatives Came* is a story about the summer that a bunch of relatives came to West Virginia for a visit. They really drove all night from Virginia and stayed for weeks. Aunts, uncles, and cousins fixed broken things, cooked and ate together, and enjoyed each other's company.

Cynthia Rylant doesn't live in West Virginia anymore, but she visits there. She likes to hear the news about the rest of her family from her grandmother. And she likes to eat her mom's corn bread. All the relatives love to see Cynthia and are proud to read her newest books.

Cynthia Rylant

STEPHEN GAMMELL

Look closely at the pictures in this story, and you will see some of *my* relatives. My wife is the photographer. (She really is one!) My dad is cutting hair, and my grandma and grandpa are gardening. Can you find me playing the guitar?

When I drew the pictures for this story, I thought about fun times I had spent with my family when I was young. Did you see the kids playing in boxes? My friends and I used to line up big boxes and then zoom away in our pretend trains and cars. It was fun!

Some of the pictures do not really have words to go along with them. I think that's what makes it fun to look at a story over and over. Every time you do, you can see something new.

Stephen Gammell

61

Families, Families

FAMILIES, FAMILIES
All kinds of families.
Mommies and daddies,
Sisters and brothers,
Aunties and uncles,
      And cousins, too.

FAMILIES, FAMILIES
All kinds of families.
People who live with us,
People who care for us,
Grandmas and grandpas,
      And babies, brand new.

FAMILIES, FAMILIES
All kinds of families.
Coming and going,
Laughing and singing,
Caring and sharing,
      And loving you.

Dorothy and Michael Strickland
illustration by Brenda Joysmith

62

Response Corner

Home Away from Home

The relatives in the story traveled a long way. Work with a partner. Pretend you own a hotel. Make up a booklet that tells about your hotel. Tell why your hotel is a good place for travelers who are far from home.

1. Pick a name for your hotel.
2. Plan what you want to say about your hotel. Tell what the rooms are like. Tell about fun things to do there.
3. Write your booklet. Include a drawing of your hotel.

Dear Relative

Write a letter to one of your relatives or to someone who lives in a place you would like to visit. Tell why you would like to go there. Name things you would like to do when you are there.

What Do You Think?

- What are some things the relatives did during their visit?
- Which would you rather do, go on a visit or have someone visit you? Tell why.

65

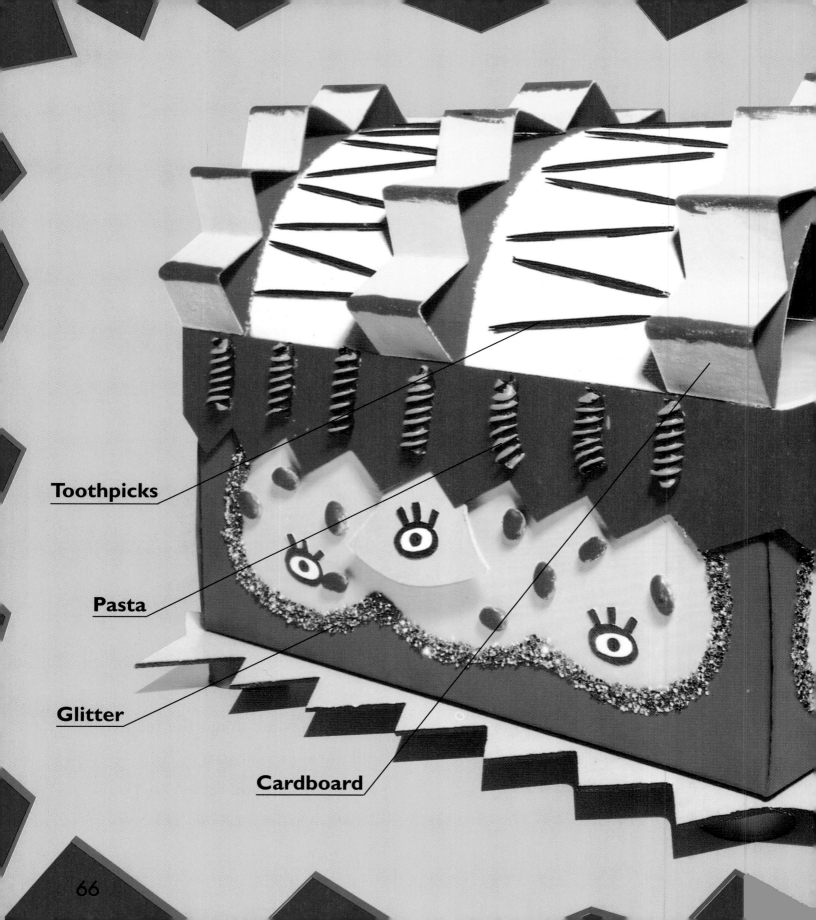

Toothpicks

Pasta

Glitter

Cardboard

FAMILY TREASURE CHEST

Pipe Cleaner

Bottle Cap

Beans

Don't Get Rid of That!

Someday you'll be glad you saved that funny photo of your sister, the first baseball card you ever traded, the feather from last year's Halloween costume. Other people might think it's junk, but to you it's family treasure. Make a chest like ours to hold your precious stuff!

ART & LITERATURE

Look at the painting by Carmen Lomas Garza. It shows the artist's family making a food called tamales. How is this family like the families you have read about? The next story you will read is about a family making tamales.

Making Tamales
by Carmen Lomas Garza

Carmen Lomas Garza paints pictures that tell stories about her childhood in Texas. She put herself in this painting. Can you see her standing next to the man in the blue overalls?

Too Many
TAMALES

by GARY SOTO   illustrated by ED MARTINEZ

Teachers'
Choice

Notable Trade
Book in
Social Studies

Snow drifted through the streets and now that it was dusk,
Christmas trees glittered in the windows.

Maria moved her nose off the glass and came back to the counter.
She was acting grown-up now, helping her mother make tamales.
Their hands were sticky with *masa*.

"That's very good," her mother said.

Maria happily kneaded the *masa*. She felt grown-up, wearing her mother's apron. Her mom had even let her wear lipstick and perfume. If only I could wear Mom's ring, she thought to herself.

Maria's mother had placed her diamond ring on the kitchen counter. Maria loved that ring. She loved how it sparkled, like their Christmas tree lights.

When her mother left the kitchen to answer the telephone, Maria couldn't help herself. She wiped her hands on the apron and looked back at the door.

"I'll wear the ring for just a minute," she said to herself.

The ring sparkled on her thumb.

Maria returned to kneading the *masa*, her hands pumping up and down. On her thumb the ring disappeared, then reappeared in the sticky glob of dough.

Her mother returned and took the bowl from her. "Go get your father for this part," she said.

Then the three of them began to spread *masa* onto corn husks. Maria's father helped by plopping a spoonful of meat in the center and folding the husk. He then placed them in a large pot on the stove.

They made twenty-four tamales as the windows grew white with delicious-smelling curls of steam.

A few hours later the family came over with armfuls of bright presents: her grandparents, her uncle and aunt, and her cousins Dolores, Teresa, and Danny.

Maria kissed everyone hello. Then she grabbed Dolores by the arm and took her upstairs to play, with the other cousins tagging along after them.

They cut out pictures from the newspaper, pictures of toys they were hoping were wrapped and sitting underneath the Christmas tree. As Maria was snipping out a picture of a pearl necklace, a shock spread through her body.

"The ring!" she screamed.

Everyone stared at her. "What ring?" Dolores asked.

Without answering, Maria ran to the kitchen.

The steaming tamales lay piled on a platter. The ring is inside one of the tamales, she thought to herself. It must have come off when I was kneading the *masa*.

Dolores, Teresa, and Danny skidded into the kitchen behind her.

"Help me!" Maria cried.

They looked at each other. Danny piped up first. "What do you want us to do?"

"Eat them," she said. "If you bite something hard, tell me."

The four of them started eating. They ripped off the husks and bit into them. The first one was good, the second one pretty good, but by the third tamale, they were tired of the taste.

"Keep eating," Maria scolded.

Corn husks littered the floor. Their stomachs were stretched till they hurt, but the cousins kept eating until only one tamale remained on the plate.

"This must be it," she said. "The ring must be in that one! We'll each take a bite. You first, Danny."

Danny was the youngest, so he didn't argue. He took a bite. Nothing.

Dolores took a bite. Nothing. Teresa took a big bite. Still nothing. It was Maria's turn. She took a deep breath and slowly, gently, bit into the last mouthful of tamale.

Nothing!

"Didn't any of you bite something hard?" Maria asked.

Danny frowned. "I think I swallowed something hard," he said.

"Swallowed it!" Maria cried, her eyes big with worry. She looked inside his mouth.

Teresa said, "I didn't bite into anything hard, but I think I'm sick." She held her stomach with both hands. Maria didn't dare look into Teresa's mouth!

She wanted to throw herself onto the floor and cry. The ring was now in her cousin's throat, or worse, his belly. How in the world could she tell her mother?

But I have to, she thought.

She could feel tears pressing to get out as she walked into the living room where the grown-ups sat talking.

They chattered so loudly that Maria didn't know how to interrupt. Finally she tugged on her mother's sleeve.

"What's the matter?" her mother asked. She took Maria's hand.

"I did something wrong," Maria sobbed.

"What?" her mother asked.

Maria thought about the beautiful ring that was now sitting inside Danny's belly, and got ready to confess.

Then she gasped. The ring was on her mother's finger, bright as ever.

"The ring!" Maria nearly screamed.

Maria's mother scraped off a flake of dried *masa*.

"You were playing with it?" she said, smiling gently.

"I wanted to wear it," Maria said, looking down at the rug. Then she told them all about how they'd eaten the tamales.

Her mother moved the ring a little on her finger. It winked a silvery light. Maria looked up and Aunt Rosa winked at her, too.

"Well, it looks like we all have to cook up another batch of tamales," Rosa said cheerfully.

Maria held her full stomach as everyone filed into the kitchen, joking and laughing. At first she still felt like crying as she kneaded a great bowl of *masa,* next to Aunt Rosa. As she pumped her hands up and down, a leftover tear fell from her eyelashes into the bowl and for just a second rested on her finger, sparkling like a jewel.

Then Rosa nudged her with her elbow and said, "Hey, *niña,* it's not so bad. Everyone knows that the second batch of tamales always tastes better than the first, right?"

When Dolores, Teresa, and Danny heard that from the other side of the room they let off a groan the size of twenty-four tamales.

Then Maria couldn't help herself: She laughed. And pretty soon everyone else was laughing, including her mother. And when Maria put her hands back into the bowl of *masa*, the leftover tear was gone.

Gary Soto

I am Mexican American, and I want to write stories that show my people and some of their traditions. In *Too Many Tamales,* I wanted to show the fun of making tamales at holiday time.

Would *you* like to be a writer? Then remember the things that happen in your life, good and not so good. You can put those things into your own stories someday.

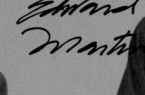

Ed Martinez

Before I painted the pictures for *Too Many Tamales,* I took pictures of friends and other models. My wife and I made *many* tamales while working on the photographs. Then everyone got to eat them!

I used warm colors in my paintings to show the warmth of this family. The bright colors help show the family's Hispanic background.

I have my own warm family—my wife, Deborah, my little boy, Oliver, and a cat named Buckwheat.

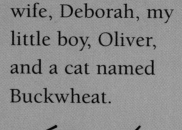

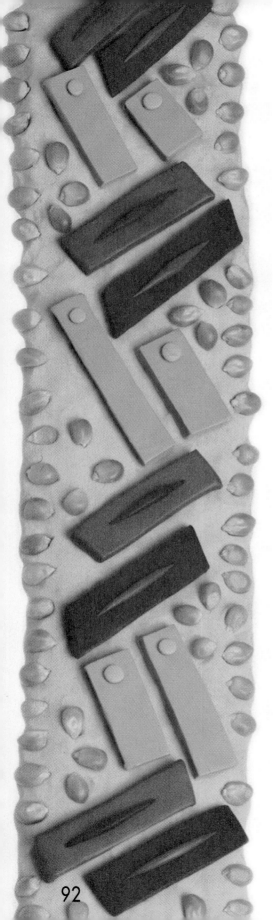

RESPONSE CORNER

Cornmeal Fun Dough

Maria's family uses cornmeal to make tamales. You and your group can use cornmeal to make a special dough.

You will need:

bowl	1 ½ cups flour
measuring cups	1 ½ cups cornmeal
self-sealing plastic bag	1 cup salt
spoon	1 cup water

1. Stir together the flour, cornmeal, and salt.

2. Add water as you knead the dough with your hands.

3. Take turns kneading until the dough is "just right" (not too sticky).

When your dough is finished, you can use it to make different shapes. Store your dough in a plastic bag.

Be a Problem Solver

Maria and her cousins ate all the tamales to try to find the missing ring. How would you have solved Maria's problem? Work with a group to find another way to solve Maria's problem.

1. Think about other things Maria could have done.

2. Choose your group's best idea.

3. Choose one person to share your group's idea with classmates.

What Do You Think?

- Why did Maria and her cousins eat all the tamales?

- Why do you think Maria didn't tell her mother when the ring was first missing?

A WORLD

Chinese people celebrate the new year on February 18. **Chinese New Year** starts off with a spring festival called **Chun Jie**. It is a time when parents and children clean and paint their homes. Everyone celebrates the new year with beautiful clothes and new shoes. The children's favorite part is eating lots of treats such as ice sticks.

Try this easy recipe and feel COOL!

ICE STICKS

You will need:
fruit juice, 1 small paper cup, tin foil, 1 craft stick

1. Pour juice into a cup.
2. Cover the top with tin foil.
3. Make a slit in the center of the foil. Put in the stick.
4. Freeze it.
   Now it's ready to eat!

OF TREATS!

Songkran is a festival to celebrate the new year in Thailand. The festival takes place in the middle of April, the hottest time of the year in Thailand. **Fruit leather** is a popular treat. Ripe fruit and a hot sun are all you need to make it!

FRUIT LEATHER

You will need:

1 pound of strawberries or other pitless fruit, water, box, cheesecloth, blender two plates, plastic wrap, pan

(Ask a grown-up to help you with steps 1 and 3.)

1. Mash the fruit in a blender.
2. Put the smooth fruit in a pan.
3. Cook on low heat until the fruit boils.
4. Turn off the stove, and let the pan cool.
5. Spread plastic wrap around each plate.
6. Spread the mashed fruit on each plate.
7. Put the plates in a box, and cover the box with cheesecloth. Then put the box in the sun. Your fruit leather will be ready to eat in 1 to 3 days.

Cinco de Mayo is Spanish for "May 5th." Cinco de Mayo is an important holiday for the people of Mexico. It is the day many years ago that Mexico became a free country. This holiday is also called Mexican Independence Day.

The Mexican children's favorite holiday treat is chocolate. Try this chocolate drink recipe, and sing the song as you stir your chocolate.

You will need:

1 ounce of chocolate
  powder (cocoa)
1 cup of cold water
a little honey
a little vanilla

Mix the ingredients in a glass, and stir with a spoon.

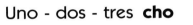

Uno - dos - tres **cho**	One - two - three **cho**
Uno - dos - tres **co**	One - two - three **co**
Uno - dos - tres **la**	One - two - three **la**
Uno - dos - tres **te**	One - two - three **te**
Cho - co - la - te	Cho - co - la - te
Bate, bate	Stir, stir
Cho - co - la - te	Cho - co - la - te

Birthdays are exciting for everyone! Kids like to have birthday parties so they can play games, get gifts, and eat treats and cake.

In the Philippines, kids celebrate birthdays in the same way. One of their favorite treats is sweet rice cakes. Try this sweet "sticky" treat, and have a **maligayang kaarawan!** ("Happy birthday!")

You will need:

1 can (about 2 cups) of sweetened coconut milk

2 cups of uncooked rice

sugar

(Let a grown-up help you with step 2.)

1. Put uncooked rice and coconut milk in a pot.

2. Cover the pot and cook the rice at medium heat for about 20 minutes.

3. Turn off the heat. Let the rice cool until it becomes a little stiff—about 10 minutes.

4. Shape 1 tablespoon of rice into a small square.

5. Sprinkle the top with sugar.

This recipe makes about 25 rice cakes.

Kwanzaa is an important time when African American families celebrate their heritage. The holiday begins on December 26 and ends on January 1. Every night until the first day of the new year, families light a candle. Also, they share a special drink from a cup called a **kikombe**.

Celebrate Kwanzaa! Make these holiday treats, and share them with your family and friends.

SENEGALESE COOKIES

You will need:
sugar cookies, already baked
peanut butter
chopped peanuts

First, spread peanut butter on top of each cookie. Then, sprinkle with chopped peanuts.

CARIBBEAN FRUIT PUNCH

You will need:

2 1/2 cups of lemonade

1 cup of orange juice

1 cup of pineapple juice

1 cup of papaya juice

1 cup of guava juice

Chill the juices. Then mix them together in a large bowl. After the juices have been mixed, pour the drink into your kikombe and enjoy!

This recipe will make about 7 cups.

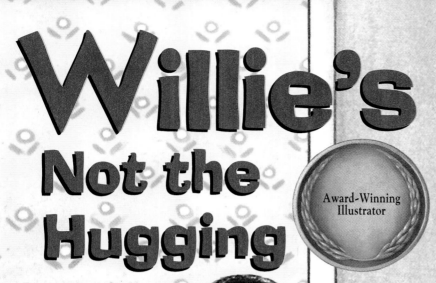

Willie's
Not the
Hugging
Kind

by Joyce
Durham Barrett

illustrated by
Pat Cummings

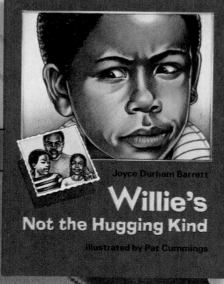

Joyce Durham Barrett

**Willie's
Not the Hugging Kind**

illustrated by Pat Cummings

Willie wanted someone to hug. That's what he wanted more than anything.

But no one hugged Willie. Not anymore.

Not even his daddy when he dropped Willie and his friend Jo-Jo off at school. Now, he just patted Willie on the head and said, "See you around, Son."

Willie didn't like to be patted on the head. It made him feel like a little dog. Besides, hugging felt much nicer, no matter what Jo-Jo said.

Every day Jo-Jo rode to school in the linen truck with Willie and his daddy. And when Willie used to hug his daddy good-bye, Jo-Jo would turn his head and laugh. "What did you do that for? Man, that's silly," Jo-Jo would say once they had crawled out of the truck.

101

So Willie stopped hugging his daddy. He never hugged his mama or his sister anymore either.

And when they tried to hug Willie, he turned away. But Willie wanted someone to hug. That's what he wanted more than anything.

At school he watched as Miss Mary put her arms around some boy or girl. It didn't look silly. Except when she tried to hug Jo-Jo. Jo-Jo made a big commotion that made everyone laugh. He wriggled and squirmed, and shrieked, "Help! Help! I'm being mugged! Help!"

At night Willie watched his sister pull her teddy bear to her and hug it. She looked so safe and happy lying there with her arms around the bear.

"Why do you hug that old thing?" Willie said. "That's silly."

Rose frowned at Willie. "Who says?" she demanded.

"Jo-Jo says, that's who says," Willie boasted.

"Well, if you ask me, I think Jo-Jo's silly," said Rose. "Besides," she said, squeezing the bear to her, "Homer's nice."

But the next night Willie pinched his nose and said, "What a smelly old bear! I wouldn't hug that old thing for a hundred dollars. Not even for a million dollars. That's silly."

Rose pulled Homer in closer to her. "Willie," she said, "you're just not the hugging kind, then . . . if that's how you feel."

Willie flipped over in bed without even saying, "Good night, sleep tight, God keep you all right." And his mind went around and around on what his sister had said. The words tick-tocked back and forth with the clock sitting on the table by his bed:

NOT-the hugging kind,
NOT-the hugging kind,
NOT-the hugging kind,
if-THAT'S-how-you-feel.

But that was not how Willie felt. More than anything, Willie wanted to be the hugging kind.

Willie watched each morning as his daddy hugged first his mama and then Rose. He remembered how safe and happy he always felt with his daddy's strong arms around him.

He remembered how good it felt to put his arms around his mama. She smelled a little like lemon and a little like the lilac powder in the bathroom. She felt big and a little lumpy. She also felt soft and safe and warm.

One morning Willie went into the kitchen and everyone was hugging everyone else. But no one hugged Willie. They didn't even see him. Willie waited, hoping someone would put their arms around him. If they did, maybe he wouldn't slip away.

But no one tried. Rose just said, when she saw Willie watching, "You know that Willie says he isn't the hugging kind now. He says it's all too, too silly."

"I did not!" said Willie, bristling. "Jo-Jo said that!"

"Oh, but you said it too, Little Brother," Rose said, laughing and tousling his hair.

Willie grabbed his lunch and his books, and ran out the door to meet Jo-Jo. "Let's get out of here!" Willie shrieked, breaking into a run. "They're mugging everybody in there!"

That afternoon Jo-Jo's mother picked him up after school, so Willie walked home alone.

He walked through the park and saw a young couple standing on the footbridge with their arms around each other.

He walked down Myrtle Street and saw a woman and a man rushing down the steps from their porch to greet some visitors with hugs all around.

It seemed so long since Willie had had a hug.

He walked into the long, low branches of a willow tree and wrapped his arms around it. A blue jay flew down from a purple plum tree, and Willie reached out to its fluttering wings. He walked up to a stop sign and hugged it.

He hugged his bike in the front yard. He hugged the door to his house when he opened it. And he rushed inside to hug his mama. But she was too busy running the vacuum over the floors. Willie was kind of glad. After all, he felt a little silly.

That night, after Willie had had his bath, he took the old bath towel and draped it across the head of his bed.

"What's that for?" Rose asked, hugging Homer to her.

"Nothing," said Willie.

The next night Willie put the old bath towel on the bed again. And the next night, and the next. Each night, when he was sure that Rose was not watching, he slipped the old towel down from the headboard and he hugged it. But it didn't feel soft and safe and warm.

Willie wanted to hug someONE, not someTHING.

In the morning Willie's mama was in the kitchen making biscuits. He watched Rose brush up to her and put her arms around her.

When the biscuits were finished and browning in the oven, Willie went up and put his arms around his mama too. Or almost around her. There was a little more to her than he remembered. She felt much nicer than an old towel. And, even better, she hugged back.

"What's all this, Willie," she said, "hugging around here on me so early in the morning?"

"Yeah, Willie," said Rose. "I thought all that hugging was too, too silly."

Willie clung tighter to his mama.

"That's all right," said his mama. "Willie knows, don't you, Son, that it's them that don't get hugging who think it's silly."

Willie looked up into his mama's face, smiling, until he felt a tap on his shoulder. Turning, he saw his daddy smiling down at him.

"My turn, Son," he said.

Willie put his arms around his daddy, burying his face in the familiar khaki shirt and feeling once again secure in the warmth of the strong arms around him.

Breakfast tasted better to Willie than it had in many a day. And when it came time to leave for school, Willie gave hugs all around.

Jumping into the big truck, Willie and his daddy stopped by to pick up Jo-Jo. When they arrived at school, Willie reached up and gave his daddy a quick, tight hug. Then he scooted out the door behind Jo-Jo.

"What did you do that for, man?" Jo-Jo said, once they were out of the truck. "Don't you know that's silly?"

Willie gave his friend a shove on the shoulder. Maybe Jo-Jo wouldn't let someone hug him, but he would allow a playful shove now and then. "Go on, now, Jo-Jo," he said. "I think *you're* what's silly."

Jo-Jo ran on ahead. "Help, help!" he shrieked. "I'm being mugged! Help!"

But Willie didn't mind. He lagged behind, feeling warm and safe knowing that he was, after all, the hugging kind.

115

Joyce Durham Barrett

Joyce Durham Barrett grew up with lots of
people to hug. She was the tenth child
in a family of eleven children. If each
child hugged every brother and sister
just once, how many hugs would that be?

Barrett is a
writer and a
school teacher.
She lives in Georgia
with her daughter.

Joyce Durham Barrett

Pat Cummings

I don't always use real people in my pictures, but I did for this story. My husband posed for Willie's father, and a friend of mine posed for his mother. I had a hard time finding a Willie. Then I met a boy named David who was perfect for Willie. A friend of David's who came along with him posed for Jo-Jo.

I started by making sketches of how I wanted each picture to look. Then I had the real people pose like the sketches. I took photographs of them. I looked at the photographs as I painted the pictures.

The pictures you see in the story were first painted with watercolors on heavy paper. Then I went over them with colored pencil. You might like to try this on some of the pictures *you* paint!

Pat Cummings

117

Send a HUG

You can send a hug through the mail if your hug is on a card!

 1 Fold a piece of paper in half. Cut it on the fold.

 2 Fold one of the strips into three equal parts.

 3 Draw an arm on the outside flap. Cut out a hand and glue it in place.

 4 Open the flap. Draw an arm on the next flap. Add a hand.

 5 Make a face that looks like yours. Cut it out and glue the head to the card.

 6 Write a special message inside the card.

me

sending you a hug
like it? I had fun
it for you.
my dog
rite back ok?
Tommy
my DOG

RESPONSE

118

It's Not Easy

Willie learned that it's not easy to hug your dad when a friend says it's silly. What other things are not easy to do? Work in a group. Make a list of everyone's ideas. Choose one idea to share with your classmates. Plan a way to share your idea.

- You can make up a short play.
- You can draw a poster.

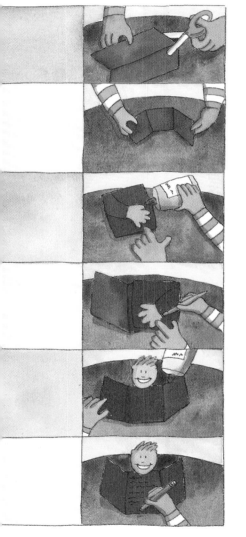

What Do You Think?

- Why did Willie let his family think he didn't like hugging?
- How did you feel at the end of this story? Why?

CORNER

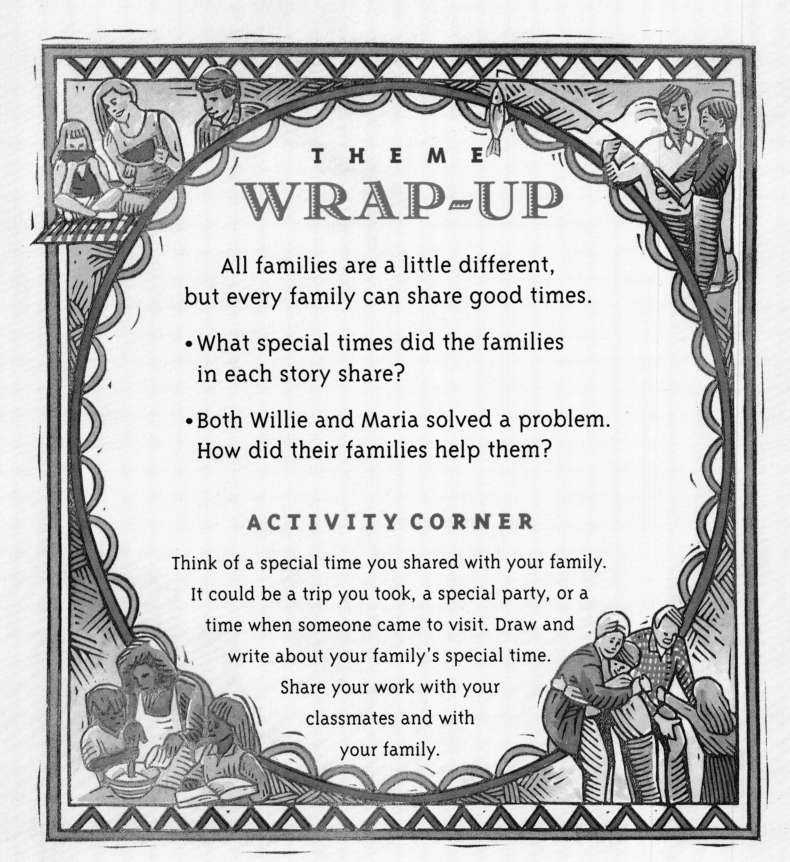

THEME
WRAP-UP

All families are a little different,
but every family can share good times.

- What special times did the families
  in each story share?

- Both Willie and Maria solved a problem.
  How did their families help them?

ACTIVITY CORNER

Think of a special time you shared with your family.
It could be a trip you took, a special party, or a
time when someone came to visit. Draw and
write about your family's special time.
Share your work with your
classmates and with
your family.

IN THE NIGHT SKY

What do you see when you look at the sky at night? On clear nights, some people look at the moon, stars, and planets. If you go outside, you might also see night animals moving about. The stories you will read will help you learn new things about stars, planets, and animals that are out at night. Then, the next time you look up at the night sky, you may think new thoughts about it.

Theme
IN THE NIGHT SKY

CONTENTS

Stellaluna

written and illustrated by
Janell Cannon

Stellaluna, a baby bat, learns about sharing and caring.

Signatures Library

Award-Winning Author

How Many Stars in the Sky?

by Lenny Hort

One summer night, a boy and his dad travel to the country to count the stars.

Signatures Library

Award-Winning Illustrator

BOOKSHELF

Alistair in Outer Space
by Marilyn Sadler

Space aliens take Alistair on a trip to outer space.

Award-Winning Author

It Came from Outer Space
by Tony Bradman

A class meets a friendly visitor from outer space. There's a surprise ending!

Award-Winning Author

Animals of the Night
by Merry Banks

When everyone is asleep, the night animals are awake—until the sun rises again.

Outstanding Science Trade Book

125

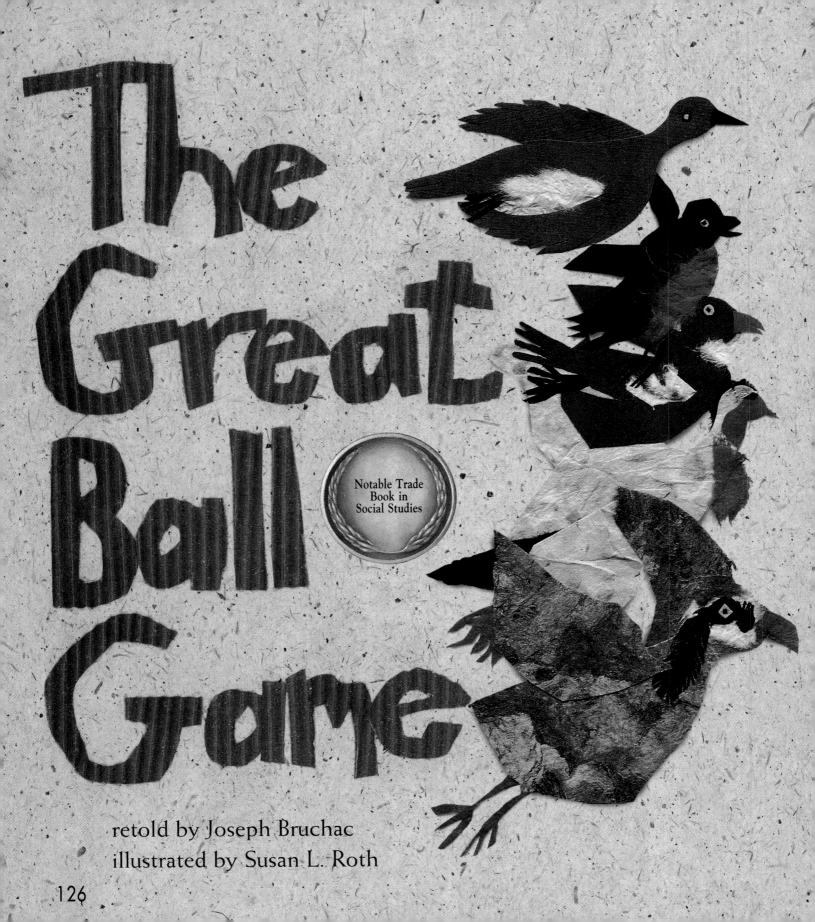

The Great Ball Game

Notable Trade Book in Social Studies

retold by Joseph Bruchac
illustrated by Susan L. Roth

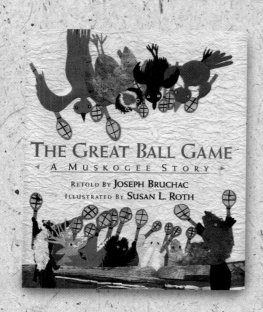

THE GREAT BALL GAME

A MUSKOGEE STORY

RETOLD BY JOSEPH BRUCHAC

ILLUSTRATED BY SUSAN L. ROTH

Long ago the Birds and
Animals had a great argument.
   "We who have wings are
better than you," said the Birds.
   "That is not so," the Animals
replied. "We who have teeth
are better."

The two sides argued back and forth. Their quarrel went on and on, until it seemed they would go to war because of it.

Then Crane, the leader of the Birds, and Bear, the leader of the Animals, had an idea.

"Let us have a ball game," Crane said. "The first side to score a goal will win the argument."

"This idea is good," said Bear. "The side that loses will have to accept the penalty given by the other side."

So they walked and flew to a field, and there they divided up into two teams.

On one side went all those who had wings. They were the Birds.

On the other side went those with teeth. They were the Animals.

But when the teams were formed, one creature was left out: Bat. He had wings *and* teeth! He flew back and forth between the two sides.

First he went to the Animals. "I have teeth," he said. "I must be on your side."

But Bear shook his head. "It would not be fair," he said. "You have wings. You must be a Bird."

131

So Bat flew to the other side. "Take me," he said to the Birds, "for you see I have wings."

But the Birds laughed at him. "You are too little to help us. We don't want you," they jeered.

Then Bat went back to the Animals. "Please let me join your team," he begged them. "The Birds laughed at me and would not accept me."

So Bear took pity on the little bat. "You are not very big," said Bear, "but sometimes even the small ones can help. We will accept you as an Animal, but you must hold back and let the bigger Animals play first."

Two poles were set up as the goalposts at each end of the field. Then the game began.

Each team played hard. On the Animals' side Fox and Deer were swift runners, and Bear cleared the way for them as they played. Crane and Hawk, though, were even swifter, and they stole the ball each time before the Animals could reach their goal.

Soon it became clear that the Birds had the advantage. Whenever they got the ball, they would fly up into the air and the Animals could not reach them. The Animals guarded their goal well, but they grew tired as the sun began to set.

Just as the sun sank below the horizon, Crane took the ball and flew toward the poles. Bear tried to stop him, but stumbled in the dim light and fell. It seemed as if the Birds would surely win.

Suddenly a small dark shape flew onto the field and stole the ball from Crane just as he was about to reach the poles. It was Bat. He darted from side to side across the field, for he did not need light to find his way. None of the Birds could catch him or block him.

Holding the ball, Bat flew right between the poles at the other end! The Animals had won!

This is how Bat came to be accepted as an Animal. He was allowed to set the penalty for the Birds.

"You Birds," Bat said, "must leave this land for half of each year."

So it is that the Birds fly south each winter. . . .

And every day at dusk Bat still comes flying
to see if the Animals need him to play ball.

139

Joseph Bruchac

Ball games have been played by Native Americans for hundreds of years. Sometimes a ball game was played to settle an argument. The two sides played the ball game instead of going to war.

This story comes from the Muskogee (or Creek) Indians. It is about how the animal people settled an argument with a ball game.

This story was told to Joseph Bruchac by Louis Littlecoon Oliver, a Muskogee Indian in Oklahoma. Bruchac made the game that is played in the story "Stickball," which is like "Lacrosse." Players of this sport have a racket in each hand for scooping up the ball. It is a game that was first played by Native Americans.

Susan L. Roth

Susan Roth used paper from all over the world to make the pictures for this story. The bright red came from an umbrella from Thailand. The dark red came from an envelope from Tibet. Some blue came from Japan and some dark green from Italy.

To make a picture, Susan Roth first lays out all the pieces on a sheet of paper. Then, she moves things around until it's just right. Finally, she glues the pieces down.

Susan Roth makes pictures for stories that come from all over the world. Some are Native American tales. Some are from Africa or India. She likes to make her pictures look like the art that the people in the story would make.

Susan L. Roth

141

Which bat hangs the highest?

The acro-bat!

Which bat knows its ABCs?

The alpha-bat!

written by **Katy Hall** and **Lisa Eisenberg**

Why did the baseball player strike out?

He was using the wrong bat!

When do bats squeak?

When they need to be oiled!

RIDDLES

pictures by Nicole Rubel

Tell a Tale with Pictures

Some Native Americans wrote stories using only pictures. Work together to retell "The Great Ball Game" in pictures. Paint your pictures on a big sheet of paper.

You will need:

mural paper, paint, paintbrushes

1. Plan who will paint each part of the story.

2. Paint pictures to tell the story. Use the pictures in "The Great Ball Game" for ideas.

3. Tell the story aloud, using the pictures.

4. Invite another class to hear your tale.

Response

Give Us a Cheer!

A great ball team needs a great cheer!
Work with a group. Choose Birds or
Animals and make up a cheer for your
team. When you are ready, you can
teach your cheer to the others.

What Do You Think?

- Why did it seem like the Birds would win?
  How did Bat help the Animals?
- Would you rather play for the Birds or the
  Animals? Why?

Corner

CREATURES
— OF THE —
NIGHT

by Judith E. Rinard

In the
evening,
as it grows
dark, raccoons go down to a river.
They are hunting for food in the
water.

Raccoons sleep during the day. But at night they wake up and are hungry. A baby raccoon slips, and almost falls. Another raccoon catches a frog and eats it.

There are many animals, like raccoons, that come out when the sun goes down. They are creatures of the night.

Flying Fox

Bats are not birds. They are
the only mammals that can fly.
This horseshoe bat searches for
insects to eat. It catches insects
in the air by scooping them up in
its wide wings. All day, bats, called
flying foxes, hang upside down in
a tree. In the evening, they will fly
off and look for fruit to eat.

Horseshoe Bat

148

Long-nosed bats feed on nectar from flowers. One laps up the sweet juice with its long tongue. The other bat pokes its head deep inside a cactus flower. Maybe it is after the very last drop of nectar.

Sanborn's Long-Nosed Bats

A flying squirrel leans out of a hole in a tree. It leaves its cozy nest when the sun goes down. Then it leaps from a high branch and spreads the flaps of skin between its front and hind legs. The flaps are like a little parachute. They help the squirrel glide down through the air.

Two squirrels peek out of their home. A third squirrel sits outside and nibbles on a nut.

A mother opossum carries her babies to a tree. The night is almost over. Day is coming, and it is time for the opossum family and other creatures of the night to go to sleep. All night, while you are sleeping, many animals are wide awake.

Isn't the world of the night a busy place?

151

The Night Stars

Douglas Gutiérrez
María Fernanda Oliver
translated by Carmen Diana Dearden

Long, long ago, in a town that was neither near nor far, there lived a man who did not like the night.

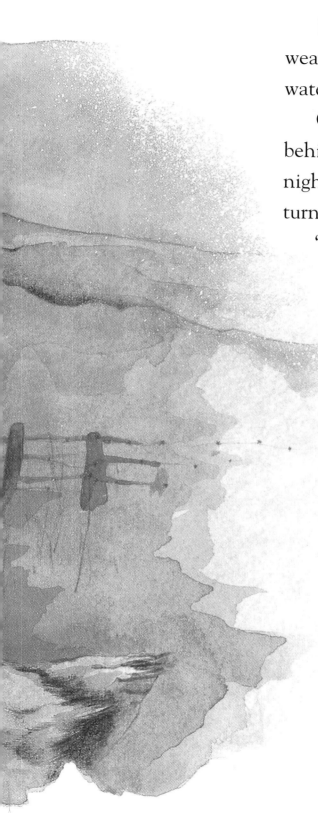

During the day, in the sunlight, he worked weaving baskets, watching over his animals and watering his vegetables.

Often he would sing. But as soon as the sun set behind the mountain, this man who did not like the night would become sad, for his world suddenly turned gray, dark and black.

"Night again! Horrible night!" he would cry out.

He would then pick up his baskets, light his lamp and shut himself up in his house.

Sometimes he would look out the window, but there was nothing to see in the dark sky. So he would put out his lamp and go to bed.

One day, at sunset, the man
went to the mountain. Night was
beginning to cover the blue sky.
The man climbed to the
highest peak and shouted:

"Please, night. Stop!"

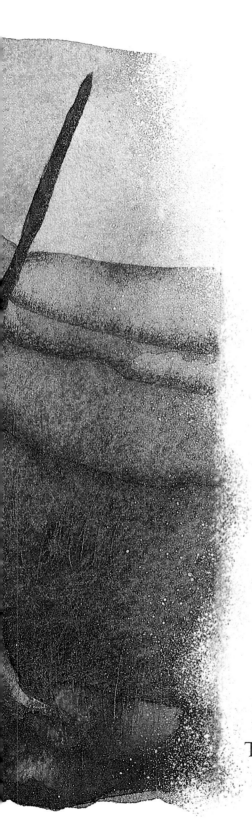

And the night did stop for a moment.

"What is it?" she asked in a soft deep voice.

"Night, I don't like you. When you come,
the light goes away and the colors disappear.
Only the darkness remains."

"You're right," answered the night. "It is so."

"Tell me, where do you take the light?"
asked the man.

"It hides behind me, and I cannot do
anything about it," replied the night.
"I'm very sorry."

The night finished stretching and covered
the world with darkness.

The man came down
from the mountain
and went to bed.

159

But he could not sleep.

Nor during the next day could he work. All he could think about was his conversation with the night. And in the afternoon, when the light began to disappear again, he said to himself: "I know what to do."

Once more he went to the mountain. The night was like an immense awning, covering all things. When at last he reached the highest point on the mountain, the man stood on his tiptoes, and with his finger poked a hole in the black sky.

A pinprick of light flickered
through the hole.
The man who did not
like the night was delighted.
He poked holes all
over the sky.
Here, there, everywhere,
and all over the sky
little points of light appeared.

Amazed now at what
he could do,
the man
made a fist
and punched it
through the darkness.
A large hole
opened up, and a
huge round light,
almost like a grapefruit,
shone through.

All the escaping light cast a brilliant glow
at the base of the mountain and lit up everything below . . .
the fields, the street, the houses.
Everything.

That night, no one in the town slept.

And ever since then, the night is full of lights,
and people everywhere can stay up late . . .
looking at the moon and the stars.

Douglas Gutiérrez

Douglas Gutiérrez lives in Venezuela, South America. He grew up near Caracas, the capital of Venezuela.

Do you like sports? Douglas Gutiérrez does! He was a gym teacher and coach for many years. He coached soccer, gymnastics, softball, and track and field.

The first book Douglas Gutiérrez wrote was about how to be a good sports teacher. *The Night of the Stars* is the first book he wrote for kids.

María Fernanda Oliver

María Fernanda Oliver was born in Venezuela, South America. *The Night of the Stars* is the first story that she has illustrated. The story was first written in Spanish. Now it can be read in English or Spanish.

María Fernanda Oliver painted the pictures with watercolor paints. Her pictures are full of colors and shapes. They are also full of feeling. Did her pictures help you understand how the man felt about the night?

167

De KOVEN

You are a dancy little thing,
You are a rascal, star!
You seem to be so near to me,
And yet you are so far.

If I could get you in my hands
You'd never get away.
I'd keep you with me always.
You'd shine both night and day.

Gwendolyn Brooks
illustrated by Joanne Scribner

168

169

RESPONSE CORNER

Night and Day

The man in the story did not like the night. Work with a partner to do an experiment about night and day.

1. Get a flashlight and a globe.

2. Put a self-stick note on the globe to show where you live.

3. Find a place that is a little bit dark.

4. One partner shines the flashlight at the globe. The other partner slowly turns the globe.

Then write a note to the man in the story. Draw pictures. Tell what you learned about night and day.

Invent a Night Remover

What might have happened if the man didn't find a way to solve his problem? Work with a partner. Invent a new product to "remove the night." Make a model of it to share with your classmates.

1. Decide what your product will be.

2. Decide how it will work.

3. Make a label that tells the name of your product and how to use it.

You will need:
a clean, empty container (a box or a plastic bottle)
crayons and markers
scissors
paper and tape

What Do You Think?

• Why did the man poke holes in the sky?

• Did this story change the way you feel about the night? Why or why not?

ART & LITERATURE

Pretend that you are walking down a street in the painting. What catches your eye as you look at the sky? How does the painting make you think of starry nights that you have seen?

The Starry Night
by Vincent van Gogh

People all over the world have enjoyed *The Starry Night*. The moon and stars seem to glow. How did Vincent van Gogh make it look as if the stars are moving across the sky?

173

SHOOTING STARS

Award-Winning
Author

Award-Winning
Illustrator

by Franklyn M. Branley

illustrated by Holly Keller

At night when the sky is clear, look for shooting stars. You can see them as soon as the sky is dark. At first you might not see any. You have to keep looking.

Lie down and gaze at the sky for an hour or so. You're almost sure to see at least one an hour. Maybe you'll see more than one. One time I saw so many, it was hard to count them.

A shooting star is not a star. Long ago people called many things in the night sky some kind of star. When they saw a planet, they called it a wandering star. They called comets long-haired stars. When they saw a streak of light, they thought a star was falling out of the sky. They called it a falling star, or a shooting star. Scientists call them meteors. The word comes from a Greek word meaning "something in the air."

If you could catch a falling star, you would discover that it is a small bit of ash, or solid material like rock or metal. It might be no larger than a grain of sand. It is called a meteoroid. When a meteoroid makes a light streak in the sky, it is called a meteor.

A meteoroid gets very hot. That's because it rubs against the air as it travels toward Earth. It gets hot, just as your hands do when you rub them together.

The meteoroid gets hot enough to produce light. That's the light you see when you see a shooting star.

Many of the meteoroids that fall toward Earth are so small that they don't make a light streak. Or they may fall during the day, when the sky is so bright that we can't see the light streak. Some scientists think that 100 tons of them fall on Earth every day. Most of them fall into the oceans. When you're outside, some of them may fall on you. But you don't feel them, because many are little more than floating specks of dust.

When a meteoroid strikes Earth, the moon, or another planet, it is called a meteorite. Most meteorites are very small. A few are as large as a marble, or even a baseball. Some are very large. One of the largest ever found is in New York City at the American Museum of Natural History. You can see it there. It was found in Greenland, where the Eskimos called it *Ahnighito*—the tent. It is mostly iron, and it weighs more than 34 tons. The Eskimos made iron knives from pieces of this meteorite.

AHNIGHITO

1982

Sometimes meteorites hit houses. In 1982 one that weighed six pounds crashed through the roof of a house in Wethersfield, Connecticut. It was traveling over 1,000 miles an hour. That was fast enough for it to go right through the ceiling and roll under the dining-room table. Eleven years earlier, in 1971, another meteorite went through the roof of a different house in the same town. That one weighed a little less than a pound.

No one was hit by either of those meteorites. But in 1954 Mrs. Hewlett Hodges, who lived in Sylacauga, Alabama, was hit in the thigh by a meteorite that came right through her ceiling. That one weighed about ten pounds. Her thigh was black and blue for quite a while.

1954

Don't worry about being hit by a meteorite. Mrs. Hodges was the first and only person in the United States ever hit by one. In the last 500 years, only a dozen people in the whole world have been hit.

Many meteorites have fallen on buildings. And many have dug deep holes, or craters, in the Earth. This crater is near Winslow, Arizona. It is 4,150 feet wide and 600 feet deep. You can walk around it and climb down to the bottom.

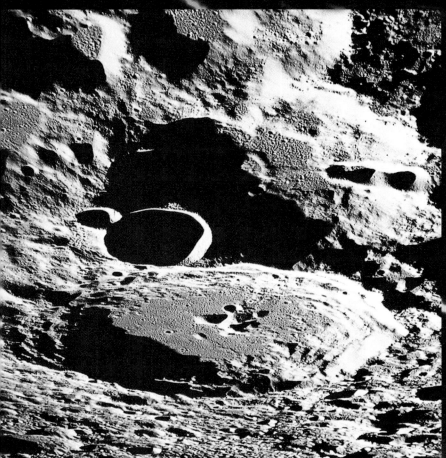

Meteorites have also fallen on the moon. In the picture, you can see that the moon is covered with craters. Many of them were made when large meteorites crashed into the moon long ago.

Mercury and Mars also have lots of craters. Many of them were dug by meteorites.

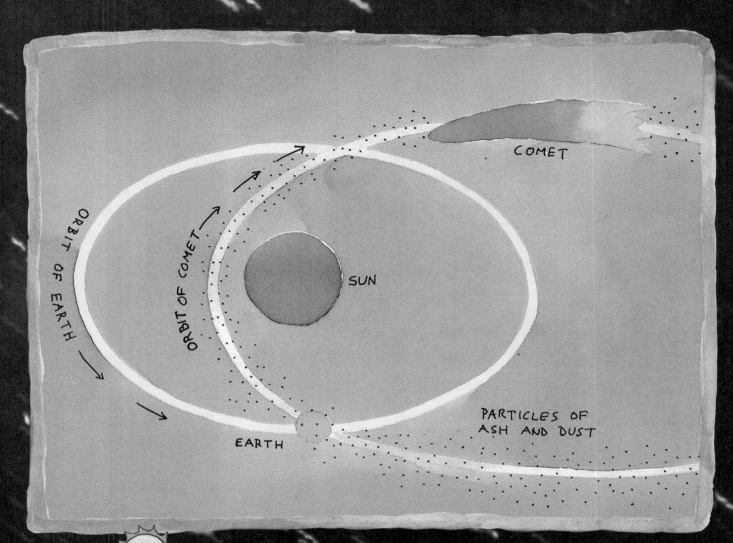

Meteorites are visitors from outer space. Billions of dust particles, stones, and rocks are in orbit around the sun. Some of them have been there since Earth began. Many of the bits of ash and dust were left behind by comets as they traveled through space. When Earth moves through clouds of these particles, they make shooting stars—sometimes so many that they fill the sky.

Keep watching for shooting stars. They seem to be far away, but most of them are less than 60 miles above the Earth. One night you may see one that seems a lot closer. You may be able to trace where it lands. You might even find the meteorite.

That's what happened in Mexico. In 1969 people saw a sky full of shooting stars. Later, almost two tons of meteorites were found by people who saw them land.

1969

Remember, at first when you look into a clear, dark sky you may not see any shooting stars. But keep watching. On a warm night, lie down and gaze at the sky. If you're lucky, you might see three or four every hour.

When you see one, make a wish. Some people say that wishes come true when they are made on a shooting star. Who knows—maybe they are right.

Franklyn M. Branley

When Franklyn Branley was an elementary school teacher, he didn't think there were enough science books for children. He decided to do something about that.

Shooting Stars is just one of over 130 fun science books that he has written. Franklyn Branley knows a lot about shooting stars because he is an astronomer. He has studied stars and planets for years. From his home by the ocean, he has seen many shooting stars.

Holly Keller

As a young person, Holly Keller had two sides—the artist and the serious student. She enjoyed learning about history in college. Later, in an art class, her teacher said that she would be good at drawing pictures for children's books. So that's what she did!

Holly Keller often writes her own stories. This is what happens when she draws pictures for someone else's story. First, someone sends her the words of the story. Then, she gets books so she can learn all about the subject. After that, she draws sketches and sends them to her editor at the book company. She also sends the pictures to an expert who makes sure they are correct. The sketches are sent back and forth until everyone likes them.

Do you know why Holly Keller likes to illustrate science books? She gets to be both an artist and a student, just as she always wanted!

Holly Keller

RESPONSE CORNER

Wish on a Shooting Star

My Pony

Once I wished for a pony.

Then I got a pony. I named him Sneakers.

WRITE A STORY

Write a story about making a wish. Your story can be about you or another character. Tell what happens after the wish is made.

After you write your story, glue it onto star-shaped paper. Add glitter. Make a galaxy of star stories on a classroom wall.

192

MAKE A BOOK

Make a Question-and-Answer book about meteorites. Each person can write one page.

Write a question about meteorites. Write the answer and draw pictures. Then put everyone's pages together, and think of a good title.

> How big are meteorites?
>
> Many meteorites are the size of marbles. →:O: Some meteorites are very big. There is a meteorite in Greenland that weighs more than 34 tons. ↓

What Do You Think?

- What is a shooting star?
- What are three facts about shooting stars that you would tell a friend?

3-2-1- BLAST-OFF!

10-9-8-7-6-5-4-3-2-1-
BLAST-OFF!

There's a burst of bright
light and huge white clouds
as powerful engines lift
the space shuttle toward
the stars.

The astronauts in the space
shuttle are special people.
Meet some of the brave
astronauts who traveled
in space.

Mae Jemison studied hard and became a doctor and a scientist. She also wanted to be an astronaut. When she was a little girl, she always dreamed about going into space. Years later her wish became real. She was chosen from a group of about 2,000 people.

Mae Jemison was the first African American woman to go into space. She blasted off on September 12, 1992, on the space shuttle *Endeavor.*

For fun, Mae Jemison dances and collects African art. Also, she appeared on the television show *Star Trek: The Next Generation.*

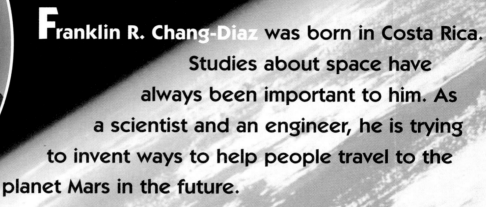

Franklin R. Chang-Diaz was born in Costa Rica. Studies about space have always been important to him. As a scientist and an engineer, he is trying to invent ways to help people travel to the planet Mars in the future.

In May 1980 Franklin Chang-Diaz was chosen to become an astronaut. His first launch into space was on January 12, 1986, on the space shuttle *Columbia*.

Robert L. Crippen became a pilot in the United States Navy. Then he became an astronaut. Robert Crippen was in the first space shuttle that lifted off into space in April 1981. He went up into space three more times after that. He was the commander of the flights. Now he is one of the people in charge of the space shuttle program.

Leroy Chiao was born in the United States. His parents are from China. He became an engineer because he was interested in science. Later he traveled to China to teach.

Leroy Chiao always wanted to do more. He is helping to build parts for future space telescopes that will help us to see different objects in space.

In July 1991 Leroy Chiao became an astronaut. He blasted off into space on July 8, 1994, on the space shuttle *Columbia*. The shuttle stayed in space for 15 days and traveled around the Earth 236 times!

Sally K. Ride is from California. She was a science teacher. Later she became an astronaut.

Sally Ride was the first American woman in space. She launched into space on the space shuttle *Challenger* in June 1983. Sally Ride went up into space again one year later. This time another woman astronaut went, too. She got the chance to be the first woman to walk in space. And she did!

Charles Bolden, Jr. became a pilot in the United States Marine Corps. Sometimes he flew planes with brand-new engines and parts to make sure the planes were ready to fly.

Because of his training as a pilot, Charles Bolden, Jr. became an astronaut in August 1981. His first trip in space on January 12, 1986, was on the space shuttle *Columbia*. He flew in space three more times. His last flight was special because it was the United States' first mission with Russia. Today Charles Bolden, Jr. is a General.

POSTCARDS FROM PLUTO

A TOUR OF THE SOLAR SYSTEM

written and illustrated by
LOREEN LEEDY

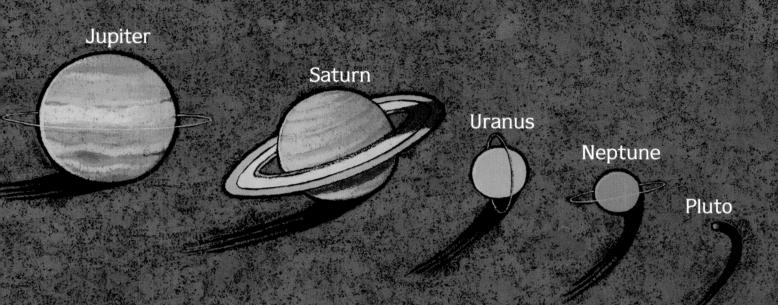

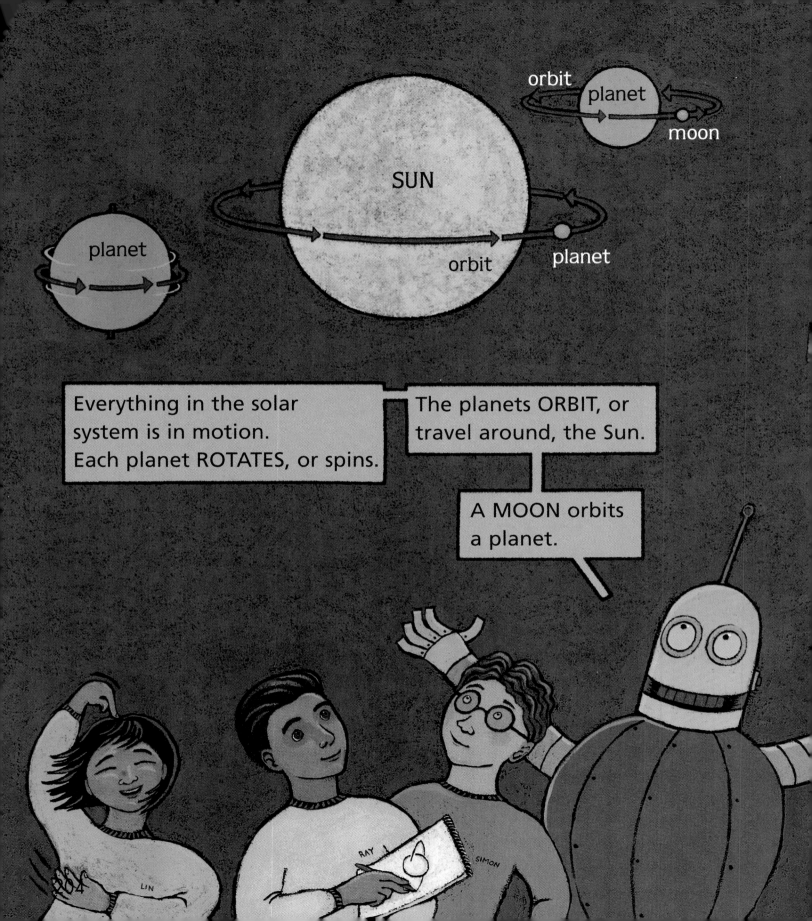

First we'll fly by the biggest, hottest, brightest object in the solar system— the Sun.

THE SUN

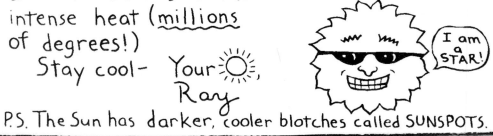

Dear Mom & Dad,
   Did U know that R Sun is really a ☆? It is only a medium-sized ☆, but over 1 million Earths could fit inside. We can't 2 close because of the intense heat (<u>millions of degrees!</u>)
   Stay cool— Your ☀,
                    Ray

Mr. + Mrs. Sol Corona
93 Shady Lane
Sun Valley, Idaho
U.S.A.   83353

I am a STAR!

P.S. The Sun has darker, cooler blotches called SUNSPOTS.

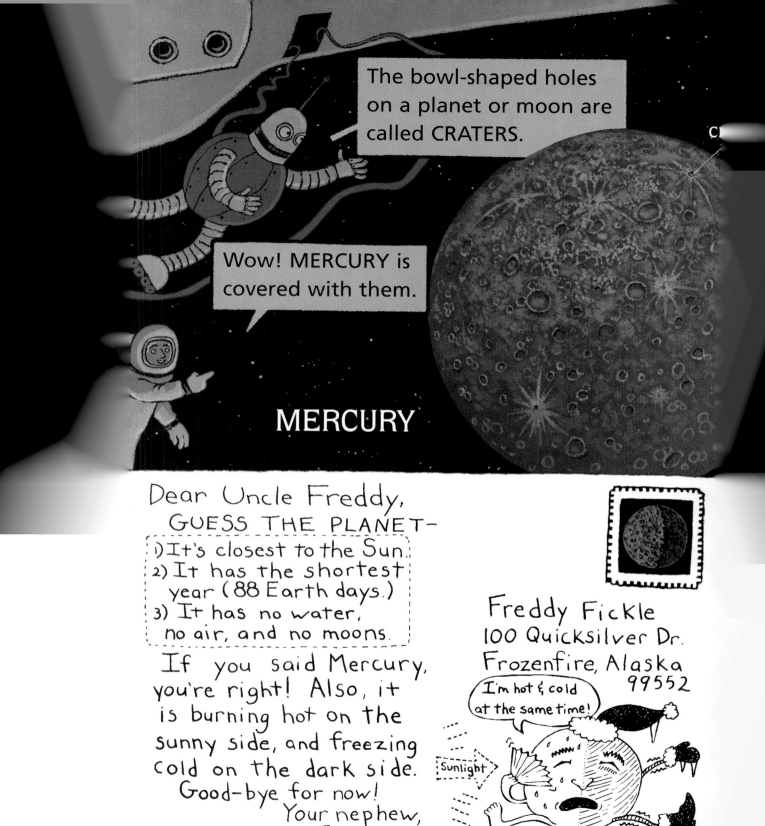

VENUS

Dear Debbie,
   We saw Venus today,
and it's a little smaller
than Earth, but much
more dangerous. It is
covered with thick, poisonous,
acid clouds. The air has
enough heat and pressure to
crack spaceships! Venus
has lots of earsplitting
thunder, and lightning, too.
   Wish you were here!
         Your friend,
         Simon

Debbie DeMilo
201 Flytrap St.
Cupid City, NY
            12420

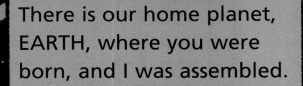

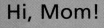

EARTH

MOON

Dear Mom,
    Guess what? We saw the actual footprints of the first astronaut to walk on Earth's moon–Neil Armstrong. We left our footprints, too.   They'll last forever because there's no wind or rain to destroy them. I guess a meteor might crash down on them. That's how the moon's craters were made. I hope a meteor doesn't land on us!
                Love,
                    Tanisha
P.S. On Earth I weigh 72 pounds– here I weigh only 12!

Luna Cee
100 Crescent Ave.
Crater Lake, OR
U.S.A. 97604

meteor

OUCH!

Earth

213

MARS

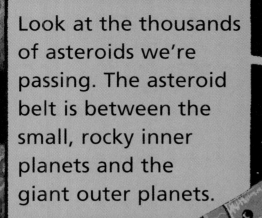

Look at the thousands of asteroids we're passing. The asteroid belt is between the small, rocky inner planets and the giant outer planets.

ASTEROID

Dear Mom and Dad,
   Dr. Quasar says that asteroids are big chunks of rock. Most of them stay in the asteroid belt, but one <u>could</u> drift out of orbit and crash into a planet (even Earth!)
     Love,
       Simon
P.S. Don't bother wearing helmets - the chance of an asteroid hitting Earth is very small.

Mr. and Mrs. Goldbloom
1000 Collision Road
Bumpers, NJ
U.S.A. 08857

THE ASTEROID BELT

Oh no!

EARTH

JUPITER is made of gases and liquids that swirl around. It has the GREAT RED SPOT which is really a huge storm.

Dear Stella,
   Did U know that Jupiter is the BIGGEST planet? It has colorful stripes, + a very faint ring system made of dust. 👁 think the weirdest thing is that 🪐 has no solid crust of land. Maybe it is sort of like melted 🍦! C U later... Your bro,
Ray

P.S. 🪐 has 16 ☾'s.

Stella Corona
93 Shady Lane
SunValley, Idaho
U.S.A. 83353

JUPITER

SATURN

URANUS

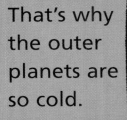

It's time to head back to Earth. I hope you all enjoyed your tour of the solar system.

Dear Mom ✚ Dad,
   Here ℝ some of the
space words 👁 learned:
ASTEROID- 🔘 space rock
COMET- ☄ chunk of frozen gas & dust
CRATER- ⌒ circular hollow
GALAXY- 🌀 huge group of stars
MOON- ☉ it orbits a planet
ORBIT- ↺ to travel around
PLANET- ⊖ it orbits a star
ROTATE- ↻ to spin
STAR- ☼ it gives off heat and light
👁 want to visit another galaxy next, okay? ♡, Ray

Mr. + Mrs. Sol Corona
93 Shady Lane
Sun Valley, ID
U.S.A. 83353

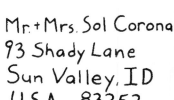

POSTCARDS FROM LOREEN LEEDY

Dear Space Traveler,

When I wrote <u>Postcards from Pluto</u>, I read all I could about our solar system. Then I decided which facts were most important. All the information had to fit on postcards like this one.

I drew the pictures for this story, too. When I make a book, I read, write, and draw pictures at about the same time. Sometimes what I write changes what I draw. Sometimes what I draw changes what I write.

I used a robot character to tie together all the facts. My robot has been around for a long time. He came from a book of mine that was never published. He just seemed like the perfect character for this story.

Happy reading!

Loreen Leedy

RESPONSE CORNER

Planets with
Personality

Look at the postcards in the story. The planets are drawn to look like people. Choose one of the planets. Paint it to look like a person. Then have a Parade of Planets.

At the end of the parade, each of you can tell your classmates about your planet.

You will need:

paints and brushes
water pan
markers or crayons
construction paper
scissors
glue or tape

1. Paint your planet.
2. Cut out the planet.
3. Add things to make the planet look like a person.

226

Write Like Ray

Look at the postcards that Ray sent.
He sometimes drew pictures of things instead
of writing words. Think of a short message you want to
send to a friend. First, write the message in words.
Write it again using pictures for some of the
words. Then, give it to your friend to read.

👁 🌙 whereU **R**

Can **U** read this? 👁

What Do You Think?

• What new things did you
learn about the solar system?

• Which planet was the most
interesting to you? Why?

Planets in Outer Space

THEME
WRAP-UP

You probably know a lot more about planets, stars, and night animals than you did before you read these stories!

- What is the most interesting thing you learned about the night?

- If you could visit a place in our solar system, where would you go? Tell why.

ACTIVITY CORNER

One of the stories you read tells why bats come out when the sun goes down. Another story tells how the moon and stars came to be in the night sky. Think of something you learned about the night. Make up a story that tells why or how this part of the night came to be.

THEME

Dare to Dream

We all dream about what we wish we could do. You might dream of dancing on stage or digging up dinosaur fossils. Your goal might be to make the world a more beautiful place. Whatever your dream is, you may have to work hard to make it come true.

CONTENTS

Dare to Dream

Tonight Is Carnaval by Arthur Dorros

Join a family as they prepare for Carnaval—a festival of singing, dancing, and feasting!

Signatures Library

Notable Trade Book in Social Studies

TONIGHT IS CARNAVAL.

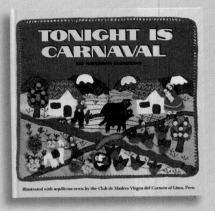

Bookshelf

Ruth Law Thrills a Nation written and illustrated by Don Brown

Ruth Law tries to fly a plane from one city to another faraway city in one day! Find out about her amazing flight.

Signatures Library

Notable Trade Book in Social Studies

Happy Birthday, Martin Luther King

by Jean Marzollo

This biography celebrates how Martin Luther King, Jr. helped bring peace to our country.

Award-Winning Author

Wanda's Roses

by Pat Brisson

The townspeople have a surprise for Wanda, whose rosebush won't bloom.

Pearl Paints

by Abigail Thomas

Pearl paints with one hand and eats dinner with the other. What will she do next?

233

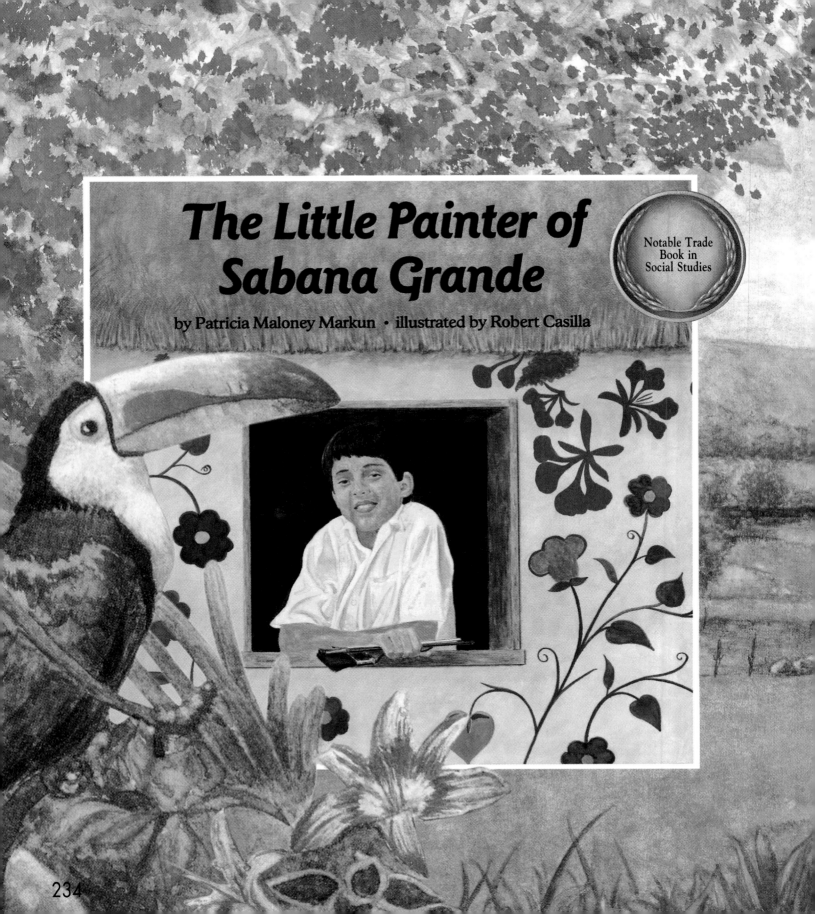

The Little Painter of
Sabana Grande

by Patricia Maloney Markun • illustrated by Robert Casilla

Notable Trade
Book in
Social Studies

High in the mountains of Panama lies the village of Sabana Grande. It is very small. Just seven houses of clay adobe stand alongside a brook in a grassy meadow. In the middle house lives the Espino family.

At dawn one cool purple morning, the rooster next door crowed. The Espinos woke up.

Papa went off to the meadow to milk the cow.

Mama stirred up the fire in the open-air kitchen and fried golden breakfast tortillas.

Fernando rolled up his straw sleeping mat and put it in the corner. He hurried to the kitchen to eat his tortilla right away.

This was an important day. At school Fernando had learned to draw colored pictures with crayons. Now school was out for dry-season vacation, and Fernando was going to paint for the first time.

His teacher, Señora Arias, had told him exactly how the country people of Panama made their paints. She said:

"Black from the charcoal of a burned tree stump.
Blue of certain berries that grow deep in the jungle.
Yellow from dried grasses in the meadow.
And red from the clay on the bottom of the brook."

It took him a long time to make the paints. Black was easy, because the burned stump of a big tree lay right next to the Espinos' adobe house.

But Fernando had to look and look before he found those certain berries deep in the jungle, to make the blue paint.

In the corner of the meadow he found a patch of very dry grass, and from that he made a large pot of yellow.

He wandered up and down alongside the brook, looking for clay. The fast-flowing water was too deep for him to reach down to the bottom. At last he came to a bend in the brook where the water was shallow. He reached down and dug up a fistful of clay. It was red, just the way Señora Arias had said.

Now his paints were stirred up and waiting—black, blue, yellow, and red, in four bowls. Next he got out the three paintbrushes his teacher had given him—one very small, one medium-sized, and one especially large.

I'm ready to paint pictures, Fernando said to himself. He picked up the small brush and dipped it into the pot of red. Then he had a terrible thought.

He had nothing to paint a picture on! An artist needs paper.

He looked in both rooms of the house. He could find no paper at all.

He ran from house to house asking everyone in Sabana Grande for paper to paint on. None of the neighbors had any. Not a scrap.

Fernando was sad. After all his work he wouldn't be able to paint pictures—the colored pictures he could almost see, he wanted to make them so badly. Paints and brushes weren't enough. He needed paper, too.

His fingers itched to draw something—anything. He
put down the paintbrush and went over to the mud by the
brook. He picked up a stick and drew in the wet dirt, the
way he had ever since he was a very little boy.

The big rooster who woke him every morning came
out of the chicken yard next door. Fernando looked at him
and drew the shape of a rooster. He sighed. He couldn't
use his new red and yellow paints to make a bright rooster.
He couldn't make the rooster's comb red. He could only
scratch out a mud-colored rooster. It wasn't the same as
painting would be. It didn't have any color.

Fernando looked around at the adobe houses of his village. Suddenly he got an idea. Adobe was smooth and white—almost like paper. Why couldn't he paint on the outside of his family's adobe house?

"No!" Papa said. "Who ever saw pictures on the outside of a house?"

"No!" Mama agreed. "What would the neighbors say?"

Fernando looked at his pots of paint and was very unhappy. He wanted to paint pictures more than anything else he could think of.

At last Papa said, "I can't stand to see my boy so miserable. All right, Fernando. Go ahead and paint on the house!"

Mama said, "Do your best, Fernando. Remember, the neighbors will have to look at your pictures for a very long time."

First Fernando made a tiny plan of the pictures he was going to paint, painting it with his smallest brush on one corner of the house.

"Your plan looks good to me, Fernando," Papa said. "If you can paint pictures small, you should be able to paint them big."

Fernando picked up his bigger brushes and started to paint a huge picture of the most beautiful tree in Panama, the flowering poinciana, on the left side of the front door. As he painted, he could look up and see the red flowers of a poinciana tree, just beginning its dry season, blooming on the mountainside.

The neighbors were very surprised.

Señora Endara called out, "Come and see what Fernando is doing!"

Señor Remon said, "Who ever saw a house with pictures on the outside?"

Pepita, the little girl next door, asked, "Does your mother know you're painting on your house?"

Fernando nodded and smiled and kept on painting. Now and then he would look up at the mountain to see the real poinciana. After a week its flowers faded and died. Fernando's tree grew bigger and brighter and redder.

On one branch he added a black toucan with a flat, yellow bill. On another branch a lazy, brown sloth hung by its three toes.

The neighbors brought out chairs. While Fernando worked, they drank coffee and watched him paint.

Next he painted the wall on the other side of the door. An imaginary vine with flat, green leaves and huge, purple blossoms crept up the wall.

Word spread about the little painter of Sabana Grande. Even people from Santa Marta, the village around the mountain, hiked into town to watch him paint. The purple vine now reached almost to the thatched roof.

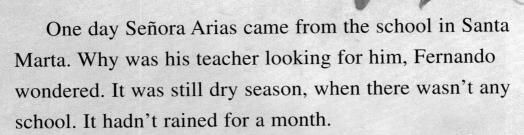

One day Señora Arias came from the school in Santa Marta. Why was his teacher looking for him, Fernando wondered. It was still dry season, when there wasn't any school. It hadn't rained for a month.

"School's not starting yet," his teacher said. "I came to see your painted adobe house that everyone in Santa Marta is talking about. Fernando, you did very well with those paintbrushes. I like it!"

She turned to the neighbors. "Don't you?"

"We certainly do!" the neighbors agreed.

They poured some coffee for the visiting teacher.

"Fernando, will you paint pictures on my house?"
asked Señora Alfaro.

"And mine, too?" asked Señor Remon.

Fernando nodded yes, but he kept on painting.

For fun he added a black, white-faced monkey looking
down at the people through purple flowers.

Next to the door he painted a big red-and-yellow
rooster, flopping its red comb as it crowed a loud "cock-a-
doodle-doo!"

Above the door he painted the words CASA FAMILIA
ESPINO, so people would know that this was the home of
the Espino family.

Now his pictures were finished. Fernando sat down with his teacher and the neighbors. Everyone said kind words about his paintings.

Fernando said nothing. He just smiled and thought to himself, There are still six adobe houses left to paint in Sabana Grande.

PATRICIA MALONEY MARKUN

This is Patricia Markun's painting, painted by the real Fernando Espino!

When Patricia Maloney Markun was living in Panama, she heard about a boy who had painted his house. So she visited his village. All of the houses were the color of sand, except one. A boy named Fernando Espino had painted colorful pictures all over his house. That very creative boy gave her the idea for this story.

Patricia Maloney Markun

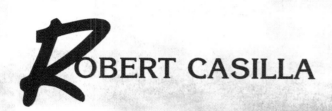OBERT CASILLA

"I love making pictures as my job, especially pictures for storybooks," says Robert Casilla. He especially enjoyed painting the pictures for *The Little Painter of Sabana Grande*. Painting the pictures of Panama reminded him of when his family lived in Puerto Rico when he was young.

This is Robert Casilla when he was your age!

"It was paradise to live in Puerto Rico. Painting these pictures gave me the chance to return there in my imagination."

Robert Casilla's favorite part of the school day was always art class. "At home, while the other kids were outside playing baseball and football, I was inside drawing and painting pictures," he says.

Robert Casilla

RAINBOW DAYS

You, whose day it is,
Make it beautiful.
Get out your rainbow colors,
So it will be beautiful.

a Nootka Indian poem

I'M GLAD...

I'm glad the sky is painted blue,
 And the earth is painted green,
With such a lot of nice fresh air
 All sandwiched in between.

Anonymous

illustrated by Terry Widener

259

Response Corner

Little Painters of Second Grade

You can paint your classroom like Fernando painted on houses.

1. Work together to plan what the picture will be.
2. Tape paper to a classroom wall. Spread newspapers on the floor.
3. Take turns painting.
4. Invite people to see your painting. Tell them about Fernando's paintings.

How-to Tips

What tips would Fernando give to someone who is painting for the first time? Think of something you know how to do. Write a list of tips for someone who has never tried doing this before.

Share your tips with classmates.

Tips for a Super Sandwich

I get out bread, peanut butter, a knife, a plate, and a banana.

I spread peanut butter on two pieces of bread.

Don't forget to peel the banana!

Slice the banana and add to one piece of bread.

Then close the sandwich.

Summertime Song

Make up a class song about things you do over the summer.

1. Sit in a circle.
2. Make up a rhythm for your song. Clap your hands and tap your legs.
3. Now say these words to your rhythm:

   What do you do in the summer time?

4. Go around the circle. Everybody claps and taps the rhythm while each person says one thing to do in the summer.

   I play ball in the summer time.

   Try not to miss a beat!

What Do You Think?

- What was Fernando's problem? How did he solve it?
- Would you like to be Fernando's neighbor? Tell why or why not.

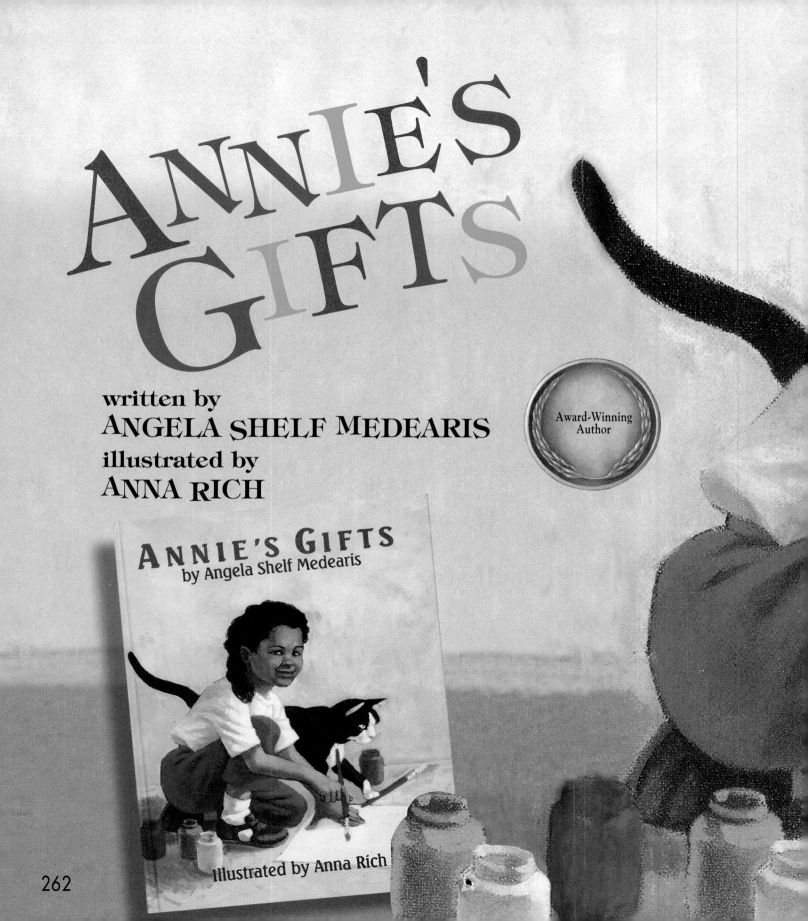

ANNIE'S GIFTS

written by
ANGELA SHELF MEDEARIS
illustrated by
ANNA RICH

Award-Winning Author

ANNIE'S GIFTS
by Angela Shelf Medearis

Illustrated by Anna Rich

O nce there lived a family
that loved music.
Every morning the children,
Lee, Patty, and Annie, turned on
some music. The floors trembled
as they stomped their feet to the
loud bass beat. Soon they were
moving down the street to catch
the school bus.

After the children left for
school, Momma would turn on
the radio. Momma swayed with
the sweet rhythm as she sipped
her coffee.

Every night, after the children were in bed, Daddy would say, "Come on honey! Let's go once around the floor." Then he and Momma slow danced to the soulful, blues music he loved.

Lee loved music so much that he joined his school band. Annie thought Lee looked wonderful in his uniform with the shiny brass buttons. Lee's music sounded like the circus. When he swung into a song on the trumpet, Annie tapped her feet and clapped her hands.

Patty was a wonderful musician, too. When Patty played the piano it made Annie think of pretty colors, soft rain, and springtime flowers. Patty also had a lovely singing voice. When company came, she would entertain the guests.

"Wonderful, just wonderful," the guests would sigh and clap their hands after Patty's performance. Annie decided that she wanted to play an instrument, too.

One day, Annie's school music teacher, Mrs. Mason, passed out instruments to the class. She gave Annie a recorder.

The class practiced a group song for months. Everyone played their part perfectly, everyone, except Annie. When Annie played, the recorder squeaked and squawked like chickens at feeding time.

"I don't think the recorder is the instrument for you," Mrs. Mason said.

"I guess you're right," Annie said. "Maybe I can play the cello."

"Let's give it a try," Mrs. Mason said. "I'll show you how to play it."

When Mrs. Mason played the cello, it sounded warm and carefree, like carousel music. Annie tried and tried, but when she played the cello, it always sounded like a chorus of screeching alley cats.

"Oh," Mrs. Mason sighed and rubbed her ears. "Annie, darling, I just don't think this is the instrument for you. How would you like to make a banner and some posters announcing our program?"

"Okay," said Annie. She was disappointed, but she did love to draw. Annie drew while everyone else practiced.

That evening, Annie picked up Lee's trumpet and tried to play it. Her playing sounded like an elephant with a bad cold. Lee begged her to stop. Annie's feelings were hurt, but she put the trumpet away.

"I wish I could find an instrument to play," Annie told her mother.

"Cheer up!" Momma said. "We're going to get a new piano and everyone is going to take piano lessons!"

Soon, a beautiful, new piano was delivered to Annie's house. The piano was made of shiny, brown mahogany. Annie peeked under the piano lid while Patty played a song. "Melody Maker" was written in beautiful gold letters.

That week, all three children started piano lessons with Mrs. Kelly. After every lesson, Mrs. Kelly gave them new sheet music to practice.

Patty and Lee did very well. Mrs. Kelly always told them how talented they were.

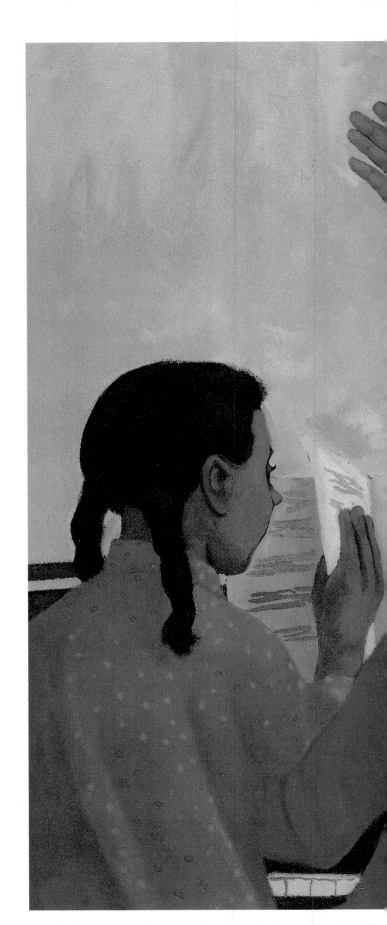

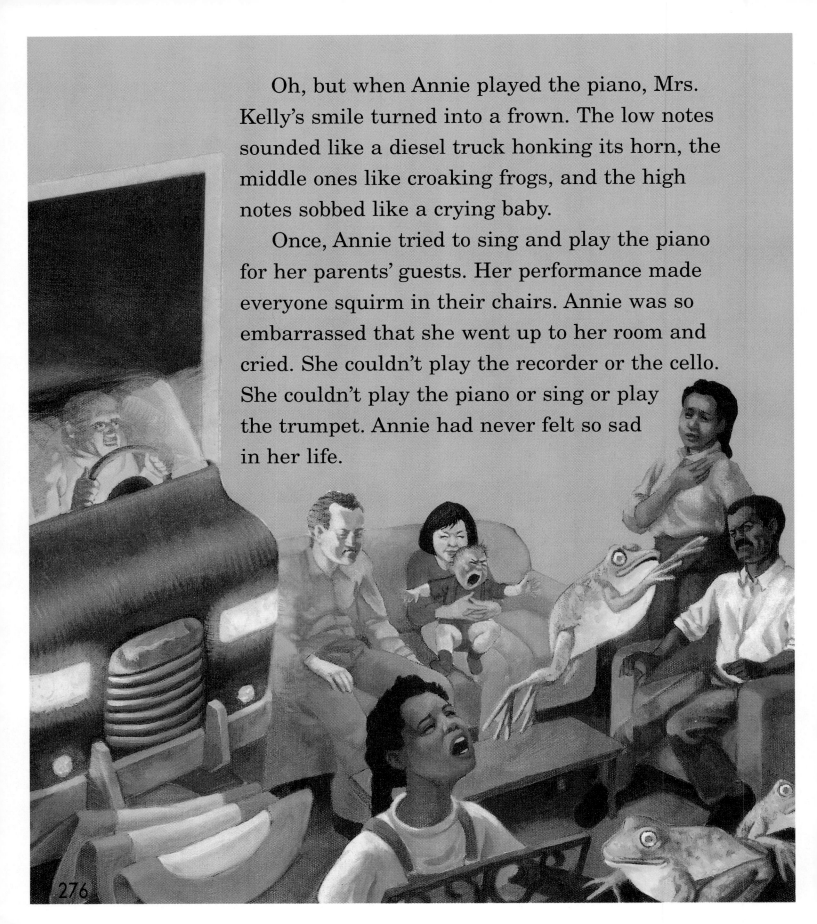

Oh, but when Annie played the piano, Mrs. Kelly's smile turned into a frown. The low notes sounded like a diesel truck honking its horn, the middle ones like croaking frogs, and the high notes sobbed like a crying baby.

Once, Annie tried to sing and play the piano for her parents' guests. Her performance made everyone squirm in their chairs. Annie was so embarrassed that she went up to her room and cried. She couldn't play the recorder or the cello. She couldn't play the piano or sing or play the trumpet. Annie had never felt so sad in her life.

Sometimes, when Annie was sad, she liked to write poetry to make herself feel better. She decided to write a poem about music.

I love to hear music play.
I practice hard every day.
But even though I try and try,
the sounds I play
make people laugh and cry.

That night, Annie put her poem on Daddy's pillow.

Then she went to sleep.

In the morning, Daddy and Momma had a long talk with Annie.

"I just can't seem to do anything right," Annie sighed.

"Yes, you can," Daddy said. "There are lots of things you can do."

"Really, Daddy?" Annie asked.

"Of course," Momma said. "Not everyone can play the piano and sing like Patty. Not everyone can play the trumpet like Lee. That's his special gift. And not everyone can write poetry and draw beautiful pictures the way you can."

"I didn't think about it that way," Annie said. "I can't sing or play an instrument well, but I can do *a lot* of other things."

Now, if you should pass by Annie's house, you might hear Patty singing and playing on the piano. Perhaps you'll hear Lee playing his trumpet. And sometimes, if you stop and listen very, very closely, you might hear Annie playing . . .

her radio!

Annie plays loud, finger-popping music when she feels like laughing and drawing pictures. She plays soft, sweet music when she writes her poems. She can play any kind of music she likes on her radio.

She still can't play the piano or sing like Patty, and she still can't play the trumpet like Lee.

But now Annie has found she's happiest when drawing her pictures and writing poetry. Because art and writing are Annie's gifts.

ANGELA SHELF MEDEARIS

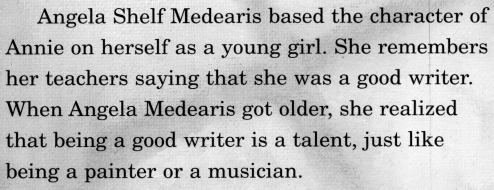

Angela Shelf Medearis based the character of Annie on herself as a young girl. She remembers her teachers saying that she was a good writer. When Angela Medearis got older, she realized that being a good writer is a talent, just like being a painter or a musician.

"I love to read. I have to read a lot because sometimes I need special information when I write my own books," says Angela Medearis. Did you know that she owns more than 500 books?

ANNA RICH

Anna Rich enjoyed making the pictures for *Annie's Gifts*. She didn't use a model when she drew Annie. She just used her imagination. Guess what? Annie turned out to look a lot like Anna!

Anna Rich says that *her* gift is the gift of art and she loves doing it. She gives this advice: "Find something *you* want to do, something to make you happy—and do it!"

This is a picture of Angela Shelf
Medearis and Anna Rich, painted
by Anna Rich. Anna Rich is sitting.

283

RESPONSE CORNER

Calling All Talent!

Art and writing are Annie's gifts. What are your gifts? Think about a special talent that you can share. Then plan a class Talent Day.

Here are some ideas:
- Plan what you will do for Talent Day.
  - Make a sign that tells about your talent.
  - Practice.
- Invite guests to come to your Talent Day.

Everybody Is Good at Something

Think about the people you know. They could be family members or friends. As you think of each person, think of something that person does well. Draw pictures to celebrate these people's special gifts. Write sentences that tell about the people and their gifts.

Picture the Music

Everyone in Annie's family loves music. They listen to it, dance to it, and some of them even play instruments.

- Listen to some music.
- Draw a picture of what the music makes you think about.
- Share your picture with a group. Did anyone have the same idea as you did?

What Do You Think?

- Why did Annie write her poem?
- Has this story changed the way you feel about your own special gifts? Why or why not?

Art and Literature

Fernando's gift is painting pictures. Annie's gifts are drawing and writing. This painting is called *Green Violinist*. How does the painting make you think about dreams and gifts?

Green Violinist
by Marc Chagall

Marc Chagall grew up in a small town in Russia. As a boy, Chagall liked to listen to his uncle play a violin. Do you think the man in the painting might be like Chagall's uncle? In what ways? What kinds of tunes do you think the *Green Violinist* might play?

I Have a Dream

I have a dream

that my four little children

will one day live in a nation

where they will not be judged

by the color of their skin,

but by the content of their character.

from a famous speech by Martin Luther King, Jr.,
at the Lincoln Memorial, Washington, D.C.,
August 28, 1963

Martin Luther King always tried to help people find peaceful ways to solve their problems. He also had a gift for speaking— when he spoke, people listened. So, he became the leader of a large group of people who helped change many unfair laws in our country.

Martin Luther King dreamed of a world where people everywhere would live together in peace. He worked hard for this dream, and so we honor him by celebrating his birthday on the third Monday in January…

Martin Luther King Day!

The Sun, the Wind and the Rain

Outstanding
Science Trade
Book

by Lisa Westberg Peters
illustrated by Ted Rand

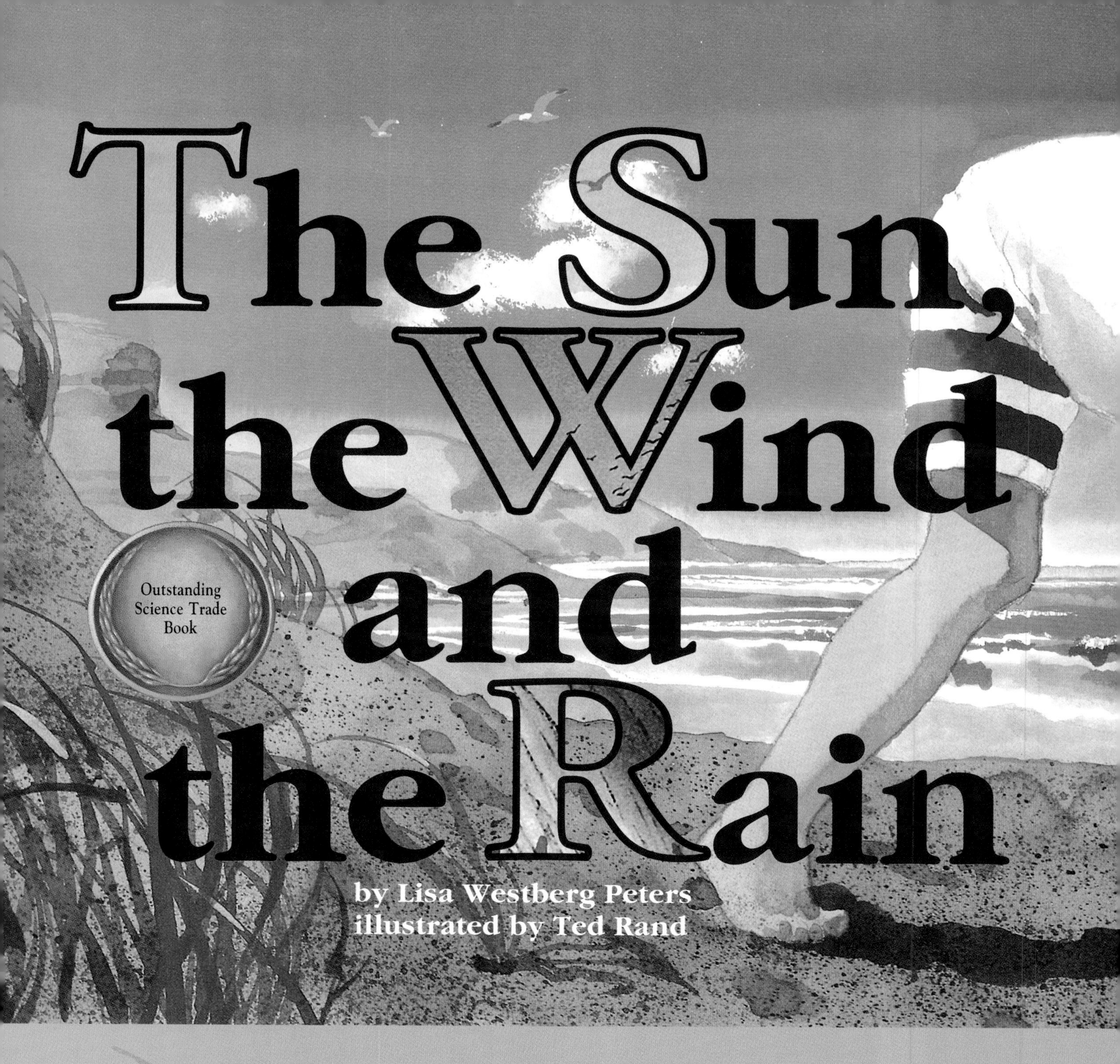

This is the story of two mountains. The earth made one.
Elizabeth in her yellow sun hat made the other.

The earth made its mountain millions of years ago. It began as a
pool underground, first fiery hot and soft, then cold and rock-hard.
Elizabeth made hers on the beach today with bucketsful of wet sand.

Eons passed. The earth cracked and shifted until the rock
of its mountain slowly rose.

Elizabeth quickly piled her sand high. She patted it smooth all the way around.

The earth mountain sparkled against the sky. Furry animals walked in its lush green valleys.

Elizabeth's mountain stood almost as tall as she, with twigs for trees and pebbles for animals. Elizabeth was proud of her fine sand mountain.

The sun beat down, day after day, year after year,
on the earth mountain's sharp peaks. The wind howled
through its canyons.

Elizabeth's mountain baked in the afternoon heat.
The breeze loosened a few grains of sand and blew them
into Elizabeth's eyes and hair.

Countless rainstorms pounded the earth mountain.
The water seeped into its rocks, making them crumble,
then tumble into small streams.

An afternoon shower blew in suddenly and Elizabeth watched as the water began to destroy the mountain she had worked so hard to build. Her tears fell as freely as the rain.

The small streams rushed together to become a raging river.
The river gouged a deep valley. It ground the earth mountain's
rough rocks into smooth pebbles.

Elizabeth could see the rain carving little valleys into
her mountain. Tiny rivers carried the sand down the beach.

As the river flowed away from the earth mountain, it ground pebbles into sand and dumped the sand on a broad plain. Then it emptied into the sea.

Elizabeth saw the sand from her mountain spread silently into small fans. She wiped away her tears.

In just a blink of earth time, the earth mountain
traded rocks for sand, jagged peaks for flat layers.

After a few minutes, the shower was over.
Elizabeth's mountain was just a bump on the beach.

The thick and heavy layers of sand sank down, down, down
into the earth until they were squeezed into layers of sandstone.

Elizabeth scooped up a handful of sand from one of the small
fans on the beach. She smiled. It was wet and hard—just right.
This time she hurried, for the sun was dropping in the sky.

The earth cracked and shifted again. Bending and breaking,
the sandstone layers slowly rose to become a new mountain.

Elizabeth finished her new sand mountain. She brushed sand
off her hands, picked up her bucket, and walked back up the beach.

Elizabeth is walking on the new earth mountain.
She steps carefully up the steep path from the beach.
When she stops to rest, she sees a smooth mound of sand
far below. It looks very small.

As she turns to leave, Elizabeth reaches out to touch the sandstone wall. Tiny grains of sand fall on her shoulders.

She brushes them off and watches them fall to the ground, where they will stay for just a while . . . in the sun, the wind and the rain.

Lisa Westberg Peters

Lisa Westberg Peters lived in Seattle, Washington, when she wrote *The Sun, the Wind and the Rain*. The idea for the story came to her after she took some geology classes and visited the mountains. She wanted to write a book to teach children the things she had learned.

Peters wanted to find a real place to use in a story about mountains. A geologist told her about a place with beaches down below and mountains up above. When she and her family visited the spot, she knew she had found the perfect place.

Ted Rand

It was lucky that Ted Rand was picked to illustrate this story. You see, he lives in Seattle, just as the author of the story did. He even spoke to the same geologist as Lisa Westberg Peters. In fact, his pictures show the exact beach that she visited with her family.

Ted Rand also used what he knows about the mountains from years of watching them. He and his wife live near the mountains. They like to hike, picnic, write, and draw pictures of their mountains.

Ted Rand likes to add little details for children to discover. Look at his pictures again. Can you find anything new?

Ted Rand

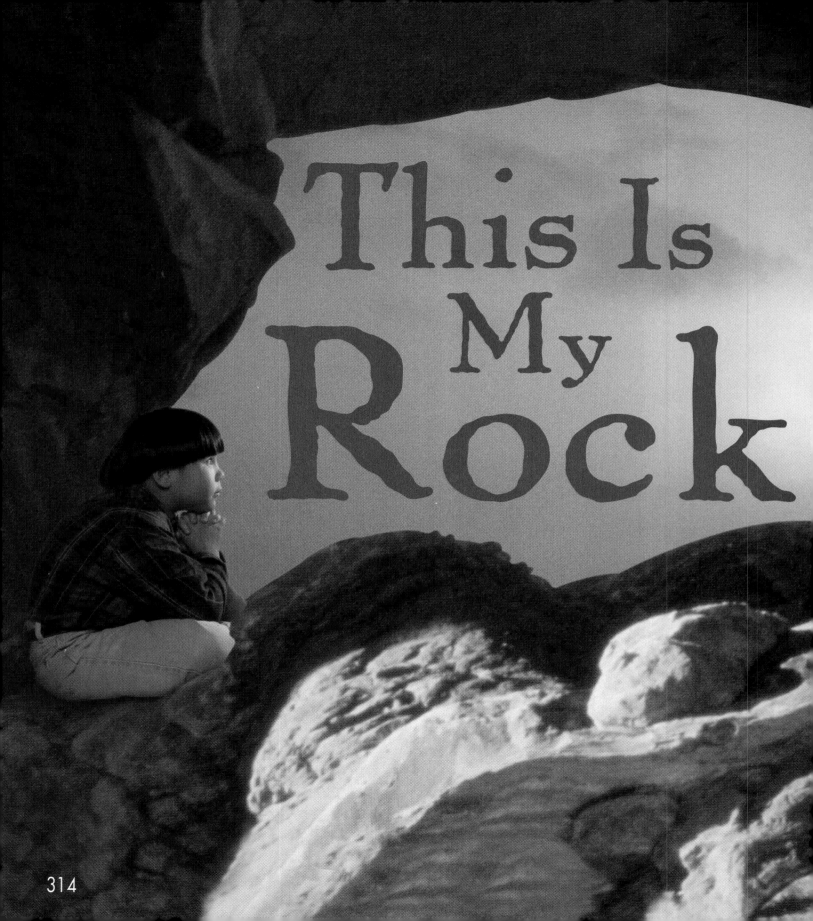

This Is
My
Rock

This is my rock
And here I run
To steal the secret of the sun;

This is my rock
And here come I
Before the night has swept the sky;

This is my rock,
This is the place
I meet the evening face to face.

David McCord

315

Response Corner

Some Things Change

The sun, the wind, and the rain change things in nature. Write a poem about other things that change.

Try using a pattern like this:

Once there was _____

Now there is _____

Some things change.

Choose a way to share your poems. You might put them into an accordion book.

Save the Earth

Look at the pictures in the story. Work with a partner. Think of ways you can save beautiful places on the earth. Make a page for a class book.

Once there was a pink blossom. Now there is a peach.

Once there was a tiny acorn. Now there is a tall oak tree. Some things change.

Once there was a caterpillar. Now there is a butterfly. Some things change.

Once there was a cloud. Now thERE is rain. Some things change.

316

Make a Mountain

You can make a mountain of clay.

1. Work with a group to make your mountain. You can add stones, twigs, and other objects from nature to it.

2. Talk with your group about how the mountain was formed. Add details to make it look real.

3. Invite younger children to see it. Tell them all about your mountain.

What Do You Think?

- How is the earth mountain like Elizabeth's mountain? How is it different?
- What did you learn about mountains that you didn't know before?

317

CHILDREN

Celebrate Earth Day every day, the Hawaiian way!

Aloha! The sun is shining, the sea is blue and the surf's up. Welcome to Hawaii where nature is bold, beautiful, and everywhere.

Meet the kids of Heeia Elementary School. They are an example of what Hawaiians call "Na Keiki 'O' Kaina" (say nah kay-EEK-ee oh kah-EE-nah). It means "Children of the Land."

With the help of Mr. Tagawa, kids at Heeia learn many important lessons about nature. They live up to their name by adopting parks and beaches to clean and beautify.

Read on and see the difference these kids are making in their environment.

318

OF THE LAND

Hawaiian Islands

Kauai

Niuai

Oahu

Moloka

Maui

Lanai

Kahoolawa

Detail of Oahu

Heeia Elementary School

Hawaii

by Rhetta Aleong

PLANT POWER

Mr. Tagawa (his students call him Mr. "T") explains how to grow native Hawaiian plants. Young *naupaka* (say now-PAH-ka) and coconut plants are kept in small pots. Then the plants are taken down to the beach for transplanting.

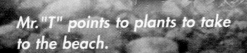

Mr. "T" points to plants to take to the beach.

Native Hawaiian plants slow down the wearing away of the beach by the sea and the wind. This is a young naupaka plant.

GET THE JOB DONE!

On clean-up day, Mr. "T" makes sure everybody gets the job done right. First, the kids clear an area of land. Then they dig holes for the rich soil and plants. The plants are put in the ground and watered.

323

Soil from the compost heap is fertilizer for the plants.

IN THE HEAP

The kids keep a compost heap at school. They dump plant and vegetable waste into large wooden boxes. After sitting in the sun and rain for a while, the compost breaks down and turns into rich soil.

Cleaning the beach is an important Earth lesson.

COLLECTORS

After planting, the class walks the beach looking for trash. They sort and collect what people thoughtlessly leave behind. Often they find things like shells, sharks' teeth and sea creatures.

GRANDFATHER'S

DREAM

Notable Trade
Book in
Social Studies

BY
HOLLY KELLER

"The new dikes are built," Grandfather announced as he dropped a piece of fish into Nam's bowl.

"Will the cranes come back now?" Nam asked. Grandfather sighed and took some rice. "We will see. Once there were so many that when they flew from the feeding ground at sunrise, they covered the whole winter sky. Then the war came, and when it was over, they were gone."

"Where did they go?"

"Safer places," Grandfather said, "and places where there was still plenty of food."

327

Mama poked the fire impatiently and turned over the last piece of fish. "Hurry and finish now, Nam," she said. "It's late. Your grandfather has made the whole village of Tam Nong worry about these birds that aren't good for anything!"

Papa patted Nam's hand. "When the rains come, the land inside the dikes will flood with water the way it always used to. The plants will grow again, and the cranes will come home."

"What if they don't?" Nam asked anxiously.

328

"If they don't," Papa said, putting down his bowl, "then the farmers will take back the land your grandfather and the others have reserved for the birds, and use it to plant more rice."

Grandfather shook his head. "And then all we will have are fat stomachs," he said angrily, and he got up from the table.

"It is past bedtime, Nam," said Mama.

Nam followed his grandfather out onto the back porch. He moved his sleeping mat close to where Grandfather was sitting, and his puppies, Cho-tom and Cho-phen, stretched out next to him.

"Grandfather," Nam asked, "why do you want the cranes to come back so much?"

"Because Vietnam was their home," the old man answered. "Cranes are strong birds and live long lives. We believed that they brought us good luck. Now the war is over, and we are all safe. The birds must be made safe, too, or they will be gone forever."

Grandfather sat for a long time without talking.

"Aren't you going to tell a story tonight?" Nam asked finally.

Grandfather smiled. "A short one," he said, "because it's late. In the old days," Grandfather began, "when there were still otters in the river, my father caught two young ones. He brought them home for me, and we fed them little pieces of cooked fish. Then my father and I trained them to catch live fish and bring them home."

"Why didn't they eat the fish they caught?" Nam asked.

Grandfather laughed. "Because we had taught them to eat only cooked fish, and they had forgotten that they were supposed to eat the live ones!"

Grandfather chuckled again as he remembered. "If the otters couldn't find a fish in the river, they would steal one. The women who were fixing dinner at the edge of the water were too busy talking to notice if a fish was snatched, and later they could never figure out what happened to their food!"

Nam fell asleep smiling, because the otter story was his favorite.

The monsoon began in the middle of May. The rain came down gently at first, and then in blinding sheets. The river swelled and the banks were flooded. The water stayed inside the dikes and did not drain off the land.

Nam spent most of his time in the house with the puppies, who were growing fast. Grandfather checked the dikes every morning, and then he sat patiently and watched the sky.

When the rains finally stopped, Grandfather got up early every morning to look for the cranes. Mama always had a bowl of steaming soup ready for him when he came home.

"Did you see any today?" Papa asked.

Grandfather shook his head. "But they will come, you'll see. Last night I was sure I heard their call."

"You are living in the past," Mama said, and she frowned. "Those birds are gone."

The days of the dry season were passing, and there was still no sign of the cranes. The village committee met and decided that if the birds did not come back before the next rainy season, the land in the reserve would be planted with rice.

Grandfather was very sad. "It was a silly dream," he said, and Nam felt sad, too.

A few weeks later Nam was in the fields watching the water buffalo. Cho-tom and Cho-phen came running across the field to play. Each dog had a small bird in its mouth.

Nam smiled. "Good dogs," he said, because he could see that the birds were not hurt.

When Nam got home, Grandfather was taking a nap.

"My dogs are just like your otters, Grandfather!" Nam called.

Grandfather opened his eyes. "Are they catching fish?"

"No," Nam said, and he laughed. "Birds, baby birds." Then Nam whispered to Papa, "The birds were gray and funny looking, and I have never seen that kind before."

Papa rubbed his chin thoughtfully, and then he put his finger across his mouth so Nam would know not to say anything.

The next morning Nam and Papa slipped out of the house before dawn. The village was dark and quiet. They reached the cranes' old feeding area just as the sun was beginning to rise. When Nam's eyes had adjusted to the pale light, he could see the cranes off in the distance.

"I have counted nearly two hundred!" Papa said.

"Can I tell Grandfather now?" Nam pleaded.

Papa nodded and pushed Nam off toward the village.

Nam couldn't get his feet to move fast enough. The sun was getting brighter, and he knew that the birds would soon be in the sky. "Come quickly, Grandfather," he shouted as he ran down the path.

He pulled Grandfather by the hand across the bridge and out toward the dikes.

In a few minutes more cranes than anyone could count flew over Tam Nong. The air was filled with their noisy call, and the whole village came out to see them.

Grandfather could hardly believe his eyes. "Aren't they beautiful!" he shouted happily.

And everyone agreed—even Mama.

That night when Nam was ready to go to bed, Grandfather sat down next to him.

"It was a good dream, after all," Nam said softly. "Do you think the cranes will stay now?"

"That is up to you," Grandfather said.

And Nam understood.

A Note from HOLLY KELLER

Dear reader,

The idea for *Grandfather's Dream* came from a trip I took to Vietnam. It all started when I read about a project to bring the cranes back to Vietnam. Cranes have always been important in that country as a symbol of long life and happy families. But, during the Vietnam War, the cranes' wetland home was destroyed. Much of the wetland was used as fields for growing rice.

My husband and I visited Vietnam with a group. We lived in a village and visited schools. We talked to the children about saving wildlife. The program worked, and the cranes are coming back!

In Vietnam we met a man who was in the war. He wants to turn his land back into wetland and save the wildlife. He told me the story of the otter and is the man on whom I based the character of Grandfather.

Holly Keller

RESPONSE CORNER

Thank You, Grandfather

If the cranes could speak, what would they say to Grandfather?
Imagine that you are one of the cranes. Make a card and write
a note inside it to Grandfather. Tell him how you feel about
what he did to bring you safely home again. You can share
your card with a partner and put it on a bulletin board.

MAKE UP A STORY

Another of Grandfather's Stories

Grandfather told Nam his favorite story, the one about the
otters and fish. But Grandfather had other stories to tell. You
can make up a story that Grandfather might have told.

- Think of a story idea. Tell your story to a partner.
- When you know your new story, draw a picture for it.
- Tell your story to classmates. Use the picture you drew.

What a Dream!

Do you think Grandfather or Nam ever dreamed about flying with the cranes? Have you ever dreamed of running, swimming, or flying with an animal? What animal would you travel with? Where would you go?

Draw a picture that shows you and your animal as you travel. Write some sentences about your dream trip.

What Do You Think?

- Why did Grandfather say that it will be up to Nam whether or not the cranes stay?
- Think about the story. Tell one way you can help nature where you live.

THEME
Wrap-Up

Some people dream of being artists. Some dream of helping our planet or other people. All of these dreams are just as important as yours!

- Fernando and Elizabeth both created something new. How were the things they made like things in nature?
- Annie and Grandfather had to work to make their dreams happen. What did each character do? How did other people help them?

ACTIVITY CORNER

What could you do to protect the earth or to make it more beautiful? Do you dream of doing something to help people? Do you know what your special gifts are? Work with a group. Make a poster about your group's dreams and gifts.

Using the Glossary

▶Get to Know It!

The **Glossary** gives the meaning of a word as it is used in the story. It also has an example sentence to show how to use the word. A **synonym,** or word that has the same meaning, sometimes comes after the example sentence. The words in the **Glossary** are in ABC order, also called **alphabetical order.**

▶How to Use It!

If you want to find *brilliant* in the **Glossary,** you should first find the **B** words. **B** is near the beginning of the alphabet, so the **B** words are near the beginning of the **Glossary.** Then you can use the guide words at the top of the page to help you find the entry word *brilliant.* It is on page 352.

This guide word is the first word on the page.

This guide word is the last word on the page.

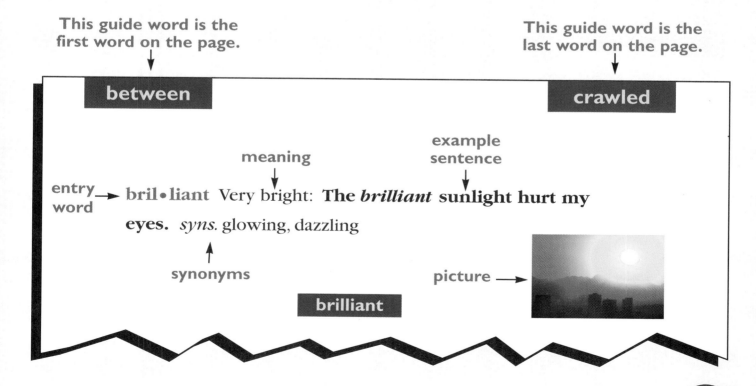

between

crawled

meaning

example sentence

entry word → bril•liant Very bright: **The *brilliant* sunlight hurt my eyes.** *syns.* glowing, dazzling

synonyms

picture →

brilliant

A

aboard

argue

artist

a•board Riding on things like ships, planes, and trains: **The people *aboard* the ship waved to the people back on land.**

ac•cept To put up with; to take: **Please *accept* this cake as my way of saying I'm sorry.**

ad•van•tage Something that helps one team do better than the other: **Our basketball players were taller, so we had the *advantage*.**

al•read•y Before a certain time: **We have *already* eaten dinner, so we aren't hungry.**

an•nounced Told others: **She *announced* the winner of the contest.**

ar•gue To give reasons for or against something: **Sometimes my sister and I *argue* about who is right.** *syns.* disagree, fight

ar•gu•ment A fight with words: **Casey had an *argument* with his friend about who was faster.** *syns.* fight, quarrel

art•ist A person who draws or paints: **The *artist* drew a picture of me.**

B

be•tween In the middle: **I sit *between* Simon and Isabel at school.**

blind•ing Making something hard to see: **The snow was so *blinding* that I couldn't see the house across the street.**

bril•liant Very bright: **The *brilliant* sunlight hurt my eyes.** *syns.* glowing, dazzling

brook A very small river: **Mom lets us play in the *brook* because the water is not deep.** *syn.* stream

bus•y Having a lot to do; working: **I was so *busy* doing my homework that I forgot my baseball practice.**

buy To use money to get something: **We *buy* food at the store.**

brook

C

cou•ple Two people together: **The *couple* sat side by side on the bench.** *syn.* pair

cov•er To hide by moving in front of: **Clouds *cover* the sun in a storm.**

crawled Moved slowly: **The cars *crawled* along the crowded city street.**

couple

351

D

dan•ger•ous Not safe: **It can be *dangerous* to cross the street without first looking both ways.**

de•li•cious Tasting or smelling good: **I love the taste of those *delicious* cookies!** *syn.* tasty

de•light•ed Very happy: **I am *delighted* that you can come to my party.** *syn.* pleased

de•stroy To wreck; to ruin: **An earthquake can *destroy* a city.** *syn.* smash

dikes Walls to keep out water: ***Dikes* were built along the river to keep the water from flooding the town.**

dis•ap•pear To go away or become hidden: **We saw the train *disappear* into the tunnel.** *syn.* vanish

dough Flour mixed with water and other things: **Uncle Ralph put the bread *dough* into a pan to bake.**

draw To make a picture: **Will you *draw* a horse for me?**

dough

F

fair Giving everyone the same chance: **The game is *fair* because everyone has a chance to win.**

fam•i•ly A group of people who are related to one another: **My *family* and I eat breakfast together.**

fi•nal•ly At last; at the end: **Ben *finally* finished his story, one week after he started it.**

flood•ed Covered with water: **After it rained, people could not drive on the *flooded* streets.**

G

goes Leaves: **After the ball game, everyone *goes* home for dinner.**

grown Bigger: **Jake has *grown* two inches since last year.**

guide A person who shows others where to go: **A *guide* showed us the way to the monkey cages.**

H

hor•ri•ble Very bad: **The food tasted *horrible*, so he would not eat it.** *syn.* awful

hours Sixty minutes: **I'm in school for five *hours* each day.**

family

353

I

instrument

in•stru•ment Something you make music on: **Would you like to play an *instrument* in the band?**

J

jeans Strong cloth pants: **Maggie wore *jeans* to the school picnic.**

L

layers

larg•er Bigger: **My dad is *larger* than I am, so he wears bigger clothes.**

lay•ers Parts that lie one on top of the other: **The baker put icing between the *layers* of the cake.**

M

meadow

mead•ow A piece of land where grass grows: **We took the sheep to the *meadow* to eat the grass.** *syns.* field, pasture

min•ute Sixty seconds; a short amount of time: **I held the frog for a *minute* and then let it go.**

mouth•ful As much as can fit in a mouth: **Tomiko ate another *mouthful* of rice.**

mu•sic Sounds you play on instruments or sing: **I like the *music* the band plays.**

N

new Not old: **Miguel got a *new* toy truck for his birthday.**

O

o•ceans Salt water that covers much of the earth: **Ships cross the *oceans* to go from one part of the world to another.** *syn.* seas

P

paint•ings Painted pictures: **Myra used red, yellow, and blue paints to make her *paintings*.**

paintings

pit•y A feeling of caring about someone who feels bad: **Peter felt *pity* for the boy who hurt his knee.**

plan•et A large, round body that goes around the sun: **The rocket flew around the *planet* Mars.**

po•em A group of sentences that often rhyme and that tell about thoughts and feelings: **Keneesha used the words <u>hop</u>, <u>flop</u>, and <u>stop</u> in her *poem* about a frog.**

planet

pound•ed Hit very hard: **The man *pounded* the nail into the wood with a hammer.**

pres•ents Things people give to one another: **Kyle got many *presents* on his birthday.** *syn.* gifts

pro•duce To make: **That factory can *produce* many new cars each day.**

Q

quar•rel A fight: **They had a *quarrel* about who would ride the bike first.** *syn.* argument

R

real Not make-believe; not fake: **Rosa read a story about a castle and then visited a *real* one.**

rel•a•tives People in a family: **I like to visit Grandma, Grandpa, and my other *relatives*.**

re•plied Said something to answer a question: **Eddie *replied* "Yes" to the teacher's question.**

S

sea•son A certain time of year: **Summer is our hot *season*.**

se•cure Safe: **During the storm, we felt warm and** *secure* **in our house.**

shoul•der A part of the body, at the top of the arm: **Jan carried the bag over her** *shoulder.*

shoulder

shove A hard push: **He gave the toy car a** *shove* **to start it rolling.**

show•er A short rain: **There was a light** *shower* **at the park, but I didn't get wet.**

shrieked Yelled in a high voice: **My aunt** *shrieked* **when the mouse ran across the floor.**

sil•ly Foolish; funny: **It would be** *silly* **to keep ice cream in a lunch box.**

shower

slow•ly In a way that is not fast: **Kent was tired, so he walked** *slowly* **down the street.**

so•lar sys•tem The sun, the planets and their moons, and other things that go around the sun: **Jupiter is the largest planet in our** *solar system.*

squawked Made a loud noise like a parrot: **The bird** *squawked* **at us when we got too close.**

stom•achs More than one belly: **Our** *stomachs* **were full from dinner.**

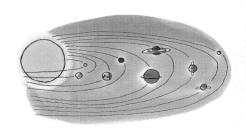

solar system

357

strange Not seen or heard of before: **We ate *strange* food when we went to a country far away.**

stretch•ing Growing: **The fog was *stretching* over the city.** *syn.* spreading

T

tend

talk•ing Speaking: **The boys were *talking* to each other on the phone.**

tend To take care of: **Let's *tend* the garden so that the vegetables will grow.**

thought Believed; felt: **Angie *thought* it was a beautiful day.**

through From beginning to end: **I read *through* the book without stopping.**

thun•der A loud noise made by lightning: **During the storm, we heard loud *thunder*.**

tour A trip to visit a place: **The class saw all kinds of animals on their *tour* of the zoo.**

U

underground

un•der•ground Below the ground: **We walked down steps to get on the *underground* train.**

V

vil•lage A small town: **Marco lives in a *village* near the top of a mountain.**

village

W

weather The way things are outside: **Do you like the cool *weather* in November?**

weighs Shows how heavy something is: **That heavy rock *weighs* fifty pounds.**

women Girls who have grown up and now are adults: **Many *women* and men took care of the children.**

women

359

Acknowledgments

For permission to reprint copyrighted material, grateful acknowledgment is made to the following sources:

Atheneum Books for Young Readers, an imprint of Simon & Schuster: Cover illustration by Ronald Himler from *Animals of the Night* by Merry Banks. Illustration copyright © 1990 by Ronald Himler.

Caroline House, Boyds Mills Press, Inc.: Cover illustration by Maryann Cocca-Leffler from *Wanda's Roses* by Pat Brisson. Illustration copyright © 1994 by Maryann Cocca-Leffler.

Children's Television Workshop, New York: "Family Treasure Chest" from *Kid City* Magazine, May 1994. Copyright 1994 by Children's Television Workshop. "Children of the Land" by Rhetta Aleong, illustration by Manuel King from *Kid City* Magazine, April 1995. Copyright 1995 by Children's Television Workshop.

Dial Books for Young Readers, a division of Penguin Books USA Inc.: Cover illustration by Carol Wright from *It Came from Outer Space* by Tony Bradman. Illustration copyright © 1992 by Carol Wright. *The Great Ball Game,* retold by Joseph Bruchac, illustrated by Susan L. Roth (adapted). Text copyright © 1994 by Joseph Bruchac; illustrations copyright © 1994 by Susan L. Roth. From *Batty Riddles* by Katy Hall and Lisa Eisenberg, illustrated by Nicole Rubel. Text copyright © 1993 by Katy Hall and Lisa Eisenberg; illustrations copyright © 1993 by Nicole Rubel.

Dutton Children's Books, a division of Penguin Books USA Inc.: Cover illustration by the Club de Madres Virgen del Carmen of Lima, Peru from *Tonight Is Carnaval* by Arthur Dorros. Illustration copyright © 1991 by Dutton Children's Books.

Greenwillow Books, a division of William Morrow & Company, Inc.: *Grandfather's Dream* by Holly Keller. Copyright © 1994 by Holly Keller. Cover illustration from *Tomorrow on Rocky Pond* by Lynn Reiser. Copyright © 1993 by Lynn Whisnant Reiser.

Harcourt Brace & Company: Cover illustration from *Stellaluna* by Janell Cannon. Copyright © 1993 by Janell Cannon.

HarperCollins Publishers: *Willie's Not the Hugging Kind* by Joyce Durham Barrett, illustrated by Pat Cummings. Text copyright © 1989 by Joyce Durham Barrett; illustrations copyright © 1989 by Pat Cummings. *Shooting Stars* by Franklyn M. Branley, illustrated by Holly Keller. Text copyright © 1989 by Franklyn M. Branley; illustrations copyright © 1989 by Holly Keller. "De Koven" from *Bronzeville Boys and Girls* by Gwendolyn Brooks. Text copyright © 1956 by Gwendolyn Brooks Blakely.

Holiday House, Inc.: *Postcards from Pluto: A Tour of the Solar System* by Loreen Leedy. Copyright © 1993 by Loreen Leedy. Cover illustration from *Who's Who in My Family?* by Loreen Leedy. Copyright © 1995 by Loreen Leedy.

Henry Holt and Company, Inc.: Cover illustration from *At the Beach* by Huy Voun Lee. Copyright © 1994 by Huy Voun Lee. *The Sun, the Wind and the Rain* by Lisa Westberg Peters, illustrated by Ted Rand. Text copyright © 1988 by Lisa Westberg Peters; illustrations copyright © 1988 by Ted Rand. Cover illustration by Margaret Hewitt from *Pearl Paints* by Abigail Thomas. Illustration copyright © 1994 by Margaret Hewitt.

Just Us Books Inc.: *Annie's Gifts* by Angela Shelf Medearis, illustrated by Anna Rich. Text copyright 1994 by Angela Shelf Medearis; illustrations copyright 1994 by Anna Rich.

Kane/Miller Book Publishers: *The Night of the Stars* by Douglas Gutiérrez, translated by Carmen Diana Dearden, illustrated by María Fernanda Oliver. Originally published in Venezuela in Spanish under the title *La Noche de Las Estrellas* by Ediciones Ekaré-Banco del Libro, 1987. Published in the United States by Kane/Miller Book Publishers, 1988.

Little, Brown and Company: "This Is My Rock" from *One at a Time* by David McCord. Text copyright 1929 by David McCord. Originally published in *The Saturday Review.*

National Geographic Society: From *Creatures of the Night* by Judith E. Rinard. Text copyright © 1977 by National Geographic Society.

Orchard Books, New York: *Shoes from Grandpa* by Mem Fox, illustrated by Patricia Mullins. Text copyright © 1989 by Mem Fox; illustrations copyright © 1989 by Patricia Mullins.

G. P. Putnam's Sons: *Too Many Tamales* by Gary Soto, illustrated by Ed Martinez. Text copyright © 1993 by Gary Soto; illustrations copyright © 1993 by Ed Martinez.

Scholastic Inc.: Cover illustration by J. Brian Pinkney from *Happy Birthday, Martin Luther King* by Jean Marzollo. Illustration copyright © 1993 by J. Brian Pinkney.

Simon & Schuster Books for Young Readers, a division of Simon & Schuster: *The Little Painter of Sabana Grande* by Patricia Maloney Markun, illustrated by Robert Casilla. Text copyright © 1993 by Patricia Maloney Markun; illustrations copyright © 1993 by Robert Casilla. Cover illustration by Cecily Lang from *A Birthday Basket for Tía* by Pat Mora. Illustration copyright © 1992 by Cecily Lang. *The Relatives Came* by Cynthia Rylant, illustrated by Stephen Gammell. Text copyright © 1985 by Cynthia Rylant; illustrations copyright ©1985 by Stephen Gammell. Cover illustration from *Jo Jo's Flying Side Kick* by Brian Pinkney. Copyright © 1995 by Brian Pinkney. Cover illustration by Roger Bollen from *Alistair in Outer Space* by Marilyn Sadler. Illustration copyright © 1984 by Roger Bollen.

Smithsonian Institution Press, Washington DC: Untitled poem (Retitled: "Rainbow Days") by Nootka, translated by Frances Densmore, from Bureau of American Ethnology, Bulletin #124.

Tambourine Books, a division of William Morrow & Company, Inc.: Cover illustration by James E. Ransome from *How Many Stars In the Sky?* by Lenny Hort. Illustration copyright © 1991 by James E. Ransome.

Ticknor & Fields Books for Young Readers, a Houghton Mifflin Company imprint: Cover illustration from *Ruth Law Thrills a Nation* by Don Brown. Copyright © 1993 by Don Brown.

Wordsong, Boyds Mills Press, Inc.: "Families, Families" by Dorothy Strickland and Michael Strickland from *Families,* selected by Dorothy S. Strickland and Michael R. Strickland. Text copyright © 1994 by Dorothy S. Strickland and Michael R. Strickland.

Photo Credits

Key: (t) top, (b) bottom, (c) center, (l) left, (r) right.

Hans & Judy Beste/ Animals Animals, 148(tl); Dennis Brack/Black Star/Harcourt Brace & Company, 141; Courtesy of Franklyn M. Branley, 190; Courtesy of Robert Casilla, 257(t); Steven Dalton/Animals Animals, 148(r)-149(l); Jack Dermid, 150(bl&r), 150(l); Courtesy of Ediciones Ekare, 167(t), 167(b); Michael Greenlar/Black Star/Harcourt Brace & Company, 140; Harvard College Observatory/ Science Photo Library/ Phot Res. Inc., 178-179; Philip Hayson/ Photo Researchers, Inc., 182-183; Dale Higgins/Harcourt Brace & Company, 91(l); Joe Johnson III, 116; Ken Karp, 170-171, 314, 317; Russ Kinne, 146(r),147(l); Russ Kinne/ Comstock, 150(b); Ron Kunzman/Harcourt Brace & Company, 225; Wayne Lankinen/ Bruce Coleman, Inc., 150(tc); Tom McHugh/ Field Museum Chicago/ Photo Res. Inc., 185; NASA, 194-196, 198; Alan G. Nelson/ Animals Animals, 146(l); Pekka Parvianen/ Science Photo Library/ Photo Res. Inc., 174-175, 192-193; Carl Purcell/ Photo Res., Inc., 180-181; Rev. Ronald Royer/ Science Photo Library/ Photo Researchers, Inc., 186-187; Jerry Schad/Photo Researchers, Inc., 188-189; Flip Schulke/ Black Star, 288-289; Joe Sohm/ Photo Res., Inc., 184-185; Mark Souffer/Animals Animals, 151(tc); Tom Sobolik/Black Star/Harcourt Brace & Company, 91(r), 117, 191, 257(b), 345; Tony Star/ World Perspectives, 197; Superstock, 199; John Troha/Black Star/Harcourt Brace & Company, 256; Merlin D. Tuttle/ Photo Res. Inc., 149(br); Steve Woit, 312; Jacqui Wong 318-323; Photos from Cynthia Rylant's autobiography "Best Wishes" copyright © 1992 published by Richard C. Owens Publishers, Inc.; Edward Potthast *A Holiday* (1915), reprinted with permission from *Children's Book Press,* SanFrancisco, California, 68-69; Vincent Van Gogh *The Starry Night* (1889), The Museum of Modern Art, New York, 172-173; Marc Chagall *The Green Violinist (Violoniste)*(1923-24), The Solomon R. Guggenheim Museum, New York, Photograph by David Heald © The Solomon R. Guggenheim Foundation, New York (FN 37.446), 286-287

Illustration Credits

Steve Johnson and Lou Fancher, Cover Art; Gyron Gin, 6-7, 13-17, 68-69, 120; Nathan Jarvis, 8-9, 121-125, 172-173, 228; Mercedes McDonald, 10-11, 229-233, 286-287, 348; Robert Casilla, 234-257; David Coulson, 194(t); Pat Cummings, 100-117; Stephen Gammell, 46-61; Iskra Johnson 174(t); Brenda Joysmith, 62-63; Kid City CTW, 68-69; Holly Keller, 174-191, 324-345; Loreen Leedy, 200-225; Ed Martínez, 70-91; Patricia Mullins, 18-43; María Fernanda Oliver, 152-167; Ted Rand, 290-313; Anna Rich, 262-283; Susan L. Roth, 126-141; Nicole Rubel, 142-143; Joanne Scribner, 168-169; Terry Widener, 258-259; Robert Casilla, 260-261; Pat Cummings 119(br); Susan Detrich, 64-65; Obadinah Heavner, 92-93; Jane Dill, 192-193; Ted Rand 316(t), 317(t&r); Loreen Leedy 226-227; Bonnie Matthews, 118-119; Rita Pocock Laskaro, 144-145; Lisa Pomerantz, 44-45; Anna Rich, 284-285; Scott Scheidly, 170-171, 284-285.